Complete Guide to Ferrets

JAMES MCKAY

SWAN·HILL
PRESS

First published in the UK in 1995 by Swan Hill Press,
an imprint of Airlife Publishing Limited
Reprinted 1998 (twice)

ISBN 185310 4337

A CIP catalogue record of this book
is available from the British Library

Typeset by Servis Filmsetting Ltd, Manchester
Printed and bound by WBC Book Manufacturers Ltd,
Bridgend, Mid Glamorgan

Swan Hill Press
an imprint of Airlife Pubishing Ltd
101 Longden Rd, Shrewsbury, England

Dedication

To Jane — still the best thing that ever happened to me –Truly!
— and to my son, James Thomas McKay, in the hope that his love of and interest in ferrets and all animals continues throughout his life.

About the Author

At the age of 16, James McKay was introduced to the delights of ferrets and ferreting by a gamekeeper, and was immediately hooked. He has remained fascinated by both ferrets and the sport of ferreting, and has done much to aid the promotion of the animal and the sport. Annoyed by the misleading public image of ferrets, he determined to put the matter right, and has been giving talks and demonstrations throughout the UK, under the auspices of the Ferret Roadshow, since 1982. In 1992, he formed the UK's National Ferret School whose aims are aptly summed up by its Latin motto, *Ut docendo fortuna viverrarum melior fiat* (Improving the ferret's lot through education).

Recognised as a leading authority on ferrets, zoologist James McKay is a lecturer in Derbyshire, where he lives with his wife Jane and their young son, Thomas, both of whom share his enthusiasm for ferrets. Previously chief executive of the UK's National Federation of Zoos, he is a Fellow of the Zoological Society of London, and an independent zoological and environmental consultant. He writes articles on pet care, wild animals, zoos, green issues and other animal-related subjects for a wide range of publications, broadcasts on radio, and regularly appears on television, both as a presenter and an informed expert guest.

Contents

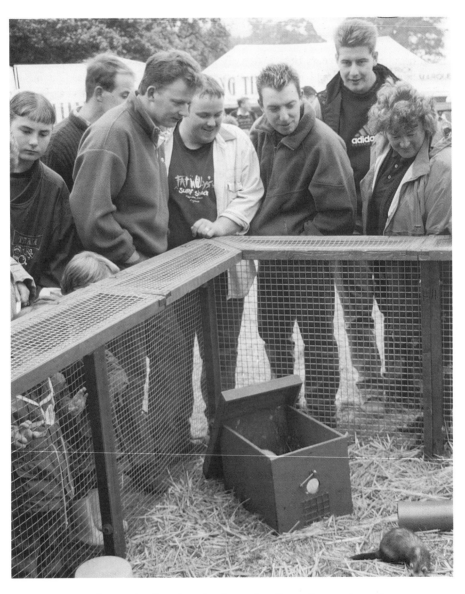

*Crowds at a display given by the author. Love them or hate them
—ferrets are fascinating!*

Introduction

Ferrets have for many years been extremely popular in such countries as Australia, New Zealand, the UK and USA, and also mainland Europe and Scandinavia, as working animals. However, people are also realising the potential of this intelligent, clean and easily trainable *mustelid* as a 'different' pet, as a 'fancy' animal, or for use in the fast growing sport of ferret racing, as well as for the more traditional uses to which the animal has been put over the years.

In the USA, where ferrets cannot be used for hunting in many states, they have long been favoured as household pets, and command quite large sums when offered for sale. Regular shows and other ferret events are organised throughout North America on a regular basis by ferret clubs and societies.

The same situation exists in Australia (where ferrets help reduce the huge number of rabbits which plague the country), several European countries, New Zealand, and all of the Scandinavian countries. In addition, large numbers of ferrets are bred — particularly in Australia and New Zealand — for their pelts (fitch fur).

In the UK, the general public have not been slow to pick up on these trends, partly due to the fact that many people will always want a pet that is different from the norm. Ferret shows and races are held throughout the country, mainly — but not exclusively — at country shows, where they have proven extremely popular and a huge crowd puller. Many ferret clubs have sprung up around the UK in the last couple of years, and now have large memberships.

A similar state of affairs exists in Europe, with ferret clubs and societies existing in almost every country. All of these clubs organise ferret shows, races and other such events, and hunting (rabbits, rats etc) with ferrets is also extremely popular in those countries where it is legal.

The ferret (and many of its relatives) has been with us as a pet, a fancy animal, and a working companion and ally for thousands of years. People love them and people hate them. However, one thing that is common to everyone is that, regardless of their own opinions on the ferret, people are still fascinated by this remarkable animal.

The subject of countless music-hall and bad-taste jokes, the ferret is a much maligned and misunderstood animal. Far from being the nasty, spiteful, untrustworthy, dirty animal that some would have us believe, the ferret is clean, intelligent, and will never bite the hand of a caring owner.

As a pet, the ferret is just as friendly as any cat could ever be, as faithful as any dog, and more interesting than any rodent or cage bird. As a working animal, the ferret shines out, as this is what nature intended for the animal. Anyone — man, woman or child — who owns and works ferrets is guaranteed sport without equal, not to mention a regular supply of good, healthy meat from the rabbits which working ferrets will hunt with such vigour.

Within the pages of this book, I intend to put right many misapprehensions, untruths and nonsense that are spoken (and written) regarding ferrets. The book is designed to ensure that everyone who has an interest in these delightful and under-rated animals is given all of the most up-to-date information available, and that every aspect of ferrets and ferreting is fully explained to all readers.

In the preparation of this book, I have had the assistance, help and guidance of many people, although naturally any mistakes are my own. I would like to express my thanks and appreciation to everyone who has helped in the writing of this book, in particular Chris Charlesworth, MRCVS, who very kindly checked and commented on the chapter on ferret diseases.

I would especially like to thank my son, Thomas, and my wife, Jane. Although not quite four years old at the time of writing, Thomas already seems to share my enthusiasm for ferrets and ferreting, and has had to see far less of me over the last few months than either of us wished, while I hammered out my manuscript on a keyboard. Jane has cheerfully endured many years of ferrets and ferreting, and the fact that I have been somewhat remiss with my attention to the household, especially the garden and the decorating!

Shortly before this book went to press, two great catastrophes struck me; thieves stole all of my ferrets and ferreting equipment, and the floppy disk on which my manuscript was stored 'crashed'.

The first catastrophe meant that thirty-five years of hard work, careful selective breeding, and painstaking record-keeping were nullified overnight. Thanks to many good friends, I now have more ferrets and equipment; some of those who had obtained ferrets from me in the past kindly returned them to me, or gave me kits from them. This means that I have *almost* got my own line back; I cannot thank those people enough.

The second tragedy meant that I had to re-write my entire book — and this was done in less than a fortnight, thanks to the patience of my family in allowing and encouraging me to devote myself entirely to the project. Luckily, I had retained all of my plans and research notes, and this made the job slightly easier, but no less galling. I now make two back-up copies of everything!

The finished item is here, and I hope that all of those who have helped me so much over the years find the contents useful and, dare I say it, instructive. My heartfelt thanks go to all mentioned, and the many hundreds who are not, but have still supported and encouraged me in my labours.

James McKay
Derbyshire, March 1995

Chapter 1

Origins

Where did ferrets originate?

You could be forgiven for believing that this is a simple question to answer; the truth is that no-one can agree — not even the 'experts'! When, why and where were they domesticated? There are many theories put forward as to the origins of the ferret and each has its adherents. Although I can offer no conclusive proof either way, I have my own ideas, and it is always interesting to examine some of the recorded facts, along with a few of the many ideas which abound concerning the pedigree of the ferret.

The first historical mention of a ferret that I can find is actually in the Bible! In Chapter Eleven of Leviticus, the ferret is listed as one of the animals which Jews were forbidden to eat. However, in some versions of the Bible, the same word is translated as weasel or even lizard, and so this reference is obviously controversial.

Aristophanes mentions the ferret in his comedy *The Acharnians*, written in about 450 BC, and Aristotle lists the ferret in his *Historia Animalium*, written about 320 BC. However, these references too are considered to be somewhat controversial, as scholars disagree on the correct translation from the Greek.

The first universally accepted reference to the ferret that I can find is that by Strabo, a Greek historian and geographer. In his book *Geographica*, written in about 20 AD, Strabo writes of an animal in Libya which was said to have been bred in captivity for hunting rabbits. He states that the animal was either used to bolt the rabbits or, if this was not possible, then the animal would hang on to the rabbit while the 'ferret', complete with captured rabbit, was dragged out on the end of its lead. If this sounds difficult to believe, then you will have even more difficulty accepting the claim that, as this animal was fastened on a line and always muzzled, it held its quarry in its claws while being dragged out on the line!

I am inclined to believe that the animal did exist (although I doubt it was actually our ferret), but that Strabo, like many modern people, did not fully understand how the 'ferret'' was actually used. Today, members of the Ruafa tribe, in Morocco, still hunt rabbits employing the services of a muzzled ferret-like animal.

Carolus Linnaeus, the Swedish naturalist and physician who, among other achievements, was responsible for 'inventing' a system of classification of all living things (first published in his botanical work *Systema Naturae*, in 1758), also seems to give credence to this reference by Strabo, as he listed the locality of the species he named *Mustela putorius* as Africa.

However, this raises several more problems in trying to establish the lineage of the ferret; neither of the animals from which most scientists believe the ferret to be descended (the European polecat — *Mustela putorius* — and the Steppe polecat — *Mustela eversmanni*) come from Africa! However, as the skeletal features of these two species most closely resemble that of the ferret, very few people would argue that one or more of these animals is not the ferret's ancestor(s).

Some authorities, however, do choose to argue, and state that the ferret is always white with red eyes (Linnaeus described the eyes as 'rubicund'), and that the animal must be kept in a warm cage, or else it will surely die from exposure, and if they escape, the ferrets will be dead within forty-eight hours. The polecat, argue these people, is an entirely different animal, as it can withstand cold and is never white. These 'facts', argue our desk-bound scientists, 'prove beyond a doubt' that the ferret's ancestors originated from the southern hemisphere. I have even read a recent book written by 'the world's leading authority on ferrets' which claims that it is unnatural and wrong for a ferret to be fed meat! This author recommends that ferrets are fed a herbivorous diet! The same author also states that ferrets love to cuddle and sleep with rabbits!!!

Other 'facts' which these people give in their published works, include the ideas that ferrets can never be tamed, are always untrustworthy, and their behaviour is always erratic, making them totally unmanageable and completely unsuitable as pets!

Those of us with real and actual first-hand experience of ferrets, however, will know that these statements about the ferret's inability to withstand the cold are utter rubbish, as the ferret is quite capable of withstanding very harsh weather conditions (although it does need a dry and draught free area in to which it can retire — in common with all other land mammals). We also know that the ferret is bred in many colours and hues, from an exact replica of the European polecat, to pure white, and every shade in between.

We know too that ferrets can live in the wild (or go feral to use the proper terminology). Feral colonies of ferrets are to be found in almost every country throughout the world; in the UK, the Island of Mull (in the Inner Hebrides) has a strong colony of feral ferrets, while in New Zealand, the ferrets have become a danger to the native fauna.

Ferrets were introduced to New Zealand in 1882, in an attempt to control the rabbit population in that country. However, the ferrets soon found that there was easier prey than rabbits. New Zealand had, until that time, had no endemic small carnivores, and consequently, the indigenous fauna had developed a unique lifestyle; many birds had evolved as flightless and ground-nesting, and these were easy prey and tasty morsels for the ferrets. Today, over twenty endemic bird species in New Zealand are suffering from the unwanted attentions of the feral ferrets on the islands. These threatened species include the kakapo, and the national bird of New Zealand, the kiwi.

There is also a feral ferret population on San Juan Island, Washington State, USA where, once again, the animal was deliberately introduced in a vain attempt to control the resident population of European rabbits. Will we never learn?

The ferret can, of course, be tamed and is *not* the sneaky character of legend. I find it vexing that, in almost every novel (or even movie) about animals, ferrets or their relatives are always portrayed as being the bad guys! Such novels include *The Wind in the Willows*, and the movie *Who Framed Roger Rabbit?*; and how many times have you read or heard the description of a nasty, sneaky thief who would sell his own mother for the price of a glass of Scotch, as being 'ferret-like'?

Perhaps this would be a good place to mention the names given to ferrets and their offspring; the males are known as hobs, although many erroneously call them dogs, while in Norfolk, England, they are known as jacks. The females are called jills, although again some wrongly refer to them as bitches, and the young (under three months) are called kits; this latter term comes from the offspring of the poleCAT — poleKITTENS. A castrated male is known as a hobble, and a vasectomised male as a hoblet. The collective noun for a group of ferrets is a business; some authorities seem to have made up their own name, and often the term 'mess' is used. This is totally incorrect. I have researched the subject thoroughly, and the earliest reference I can find to collective nouns of animals is in a book written by Dame Juliana Bernes, *The Boke of St Albans*, which contains a list of 'the companys of beestys and fowleys' (*sic*). The term given in this book, printed in 1468, is a '*besynes of ferrettis*'; there can be no mistaking the updating of that term to 'a business of ferrets'! I am also certain that terms such as this are given for good reason; they often accurately describe the nature of the species. Anyone who has ever witnessed two or three ferrets turned loose together, will tell you that they certainly get on with their business of ferreting things out, without any prompting or encouragement!

Of course, the very name ferret will help establish the animal's perceived character, as it comes from the Latin *furonem*, which means thief (hence the word *furo*, often put as the third part of the ferret's scientific name). Today, ferret is also used as a verb, meaning to search diligently, to remove from a hiding place, or to draw out by shrewd questioning; a military vehicle, used for reconnaissance and scouting purposes, also has the name 'Ferret'. Built by Alvis in the UK, the company obviously chose the name very carefully, and the vehicle, currently in service with the armies and security services of many countries world-wide, lives up to the reputation of the real ferret.

Other names for the ferret and its wild relatives include fitch, fitchet, poley, stinkmart, stinkmarten, foulmart, foulmarten, foumart and fulimart. Most of these names help signify the smell of the ferret; even the most ardent fan of the animal cannot but agree that the ferret does have a very characteristic smell!

'Poley', 'polecat ferret', 'fitch' and 'fitchet' were terms originally given to a hybrid of the wild polecat and its domesticated cousin, the ferret. Today, however, the terms are used to describe any ferret which resembles the polecat, ie has polecat markings. Legends about hybrids of ferrets and polecats abound; some will tell you that the two animals cannot produce offspring. Others will tell you that any offspring from such a mating will be infertile; some will tell you that kits from polecat to ferret matings are easy to spot, but impossible to tame. Although all of the foregoing 'facts' are totally wrong, almost everyone will tell you that they have gained this knowledge from first-hand experience; I have never yet met an 'experienced ferreter' who does not claim to have had (or still got) a *true* polecat. When questioned, however, the source of this 'polecat' is always obscure and unbelievable. I am convinced that, in ninety-nine point nine per cent of cases, the 'true polecat' is simply a large, dark-coloured ferret with polecat colouring. I refer to all polecats and/or ferrets kept in captivity simply as ferrets.

Having said that, I too claim to have a true polecat. I obtained my specimen, a hob named Rasputin, from a British zoo; its ancestors had been taken into captivity around the turn of the century, having been bought from a gamekeeper who had trapped them. Since that day, no other animals have been introduced to the colony, and so they are as true a polecat as we are likely to find. It is worthy of note that, when scientists carried out genetic investigations on wild polecats, they found that many of them were hybridised with feral ferrets.

Rasputin, by-the-way, is now in the care of a great friend of mine, Arthur Bates, who lives near Chesterfield. Between us, Arthur and I have used Rasputin to father many kits; they are all healthy, fertile (many are parents and grandparents themselves), and tame. People from many miles around visit Arthur to buy Rasputin's kits, or have their jills mated by the amiable polecat hob.

The name polecat gives an indication of the ferret's propensity for stealing; it comes from the French *poulechat*, meaning 'chicken (killing) cat'.

No-one with first-hand experience of ferrets could possibly deny that ferrets *do* make excellent pets, providing that the owner makes the time and takes the effort to handle their charges regularly, and treat them well. My own ferrets will come to my call, walk along at my heels, and love having their tummy tickled! I allow my son (currently three years of age) to handle and play with all of our ferrets when we are around to supervise, and he has never been bitten or attacked in any way by the ferrets — even when he interrupts or joins in their games of 'chase'. The same ferrets, however, will willingly and effectively flush rabbits from their underground home.

Pliny the Elder (Gaius Plinius Secundus), the Roman scientist and historian, wrote many books, some of which survived his fate (he was killed in the eruption of Mount Vesuvius in 79 AD). The subjects covered by these books were geography, astronomy, and natural history. One of these books, *Natural History*, mentions both the ferret and the rabbit, and there are many more such references in his book.

Isidore of Seville, a writer and missionary, who was appointed as Bishop of Seville, Spain, in 600 AD, wrote many important books, including his *Ethymologiae*, the model for later medieval encyclopedias. In his book *Patrologie*, written about 600 AD, he wrote of the ferret's use in rabbit hunting.

It is not known for certain when the first 'ferret' (or more correctly semi-tame polecat), was introduced into Great Britain, but I'm sure that it must have been linked with the introduction of another foreign invader — the rabbit. The rabbit, whose history is intertwined and inexorably linked with that of the ferret, was originally indigenous to Spain and North Africa but, by the end of the first century AD, was firmly ensconced in southern France.

Until the Roman period, the rabbit was restricted to an area encompassing the Iberian Peninsular (Spain), North Africa and southern France; some scientists believe that, if the rabbit had not been introduced to Europe, then it would have shared the same fate as the European pika, and become extinct. So although most species can blame man for their untimely demise and suffering, the rabbit is one of a select group of mammals (which include the horse and the dog) whose widespread distribution and success owes much to the activities of *Homo sapiens.*

The Romans were responsible for the rabbit's spread from Spain, but they did not make any attempt at domesticating the species; instead they chose simply to catch the rabbits and fatten them for the table, or leave them to live in the wild until needed for their culinary delights. For convenience sake, the Romans kept many rabbits in artificial areas (ie warrens), until they were taken for the pot. However, as everyone knows, rabbits are accomplished burrowers, and it was not long before many made their escape, thus colonising new areas. Most authorities (although not all) agree that the rabbit did not reach Britain's shores until Norman times.

The selective breeding of rabbits was probably first carried out by monks, who regarded the newly-born and unborn rabbit kittens as 'not meat'; this convenient classification enabled the monks to eat the rabbit kittens during 'fasts'. However, the monks' rabbits, kept in walled and paved areas for convenient harvesting, also escaped, and this helped to spread the wild population even more.

To try to combat these escapes, many land owners in the Middle Ages established rabbit colonies on islands, where the animals (and their spread) could easily be controlled. Ships also carried rabbits with them on long voyages, and left small colonies on the islands that they stopped at, as a food source to tap in to every time they were in the area. This latter practice led to devastation on some islands, with the indigenous species being wiped out due to the habits of the rabbit. One of the best (or worst!) examples of this was Round Island, near Mauritius.

In the 1970s, the island was in a diabolical state, due mainly to the rabbits and goats put there by man, presumably for food supplies. Many of the endemic species were in danger of imminent extinction and, had it not been for the sterling efforts of Gerald Durrell and the Jersey Wildlife Preservation Trust, these species would have joined the dodo and countless other species driven down the one-way road to oblivion that is extinction — and extinction is for ever! At the time of writing (February 1994), Round Island is, thanks to Gerald Durrell and his helpers, on its way to recovery, following extensive trapping and shooting of the foreign invaders, thus clearing the way for the island's indigenous species to re-colonise the land. This has only been possible because of captive breeding in establishments like Jersey Zoo; if ever you were in any doubt about the need for zoos in the twentieth and twenty-first centuries, this surely is proof.

By the Middle Ages, the ferret was widely used for hunting the rabbit, and many references to this practice still exist in historical records. Queen Mary's Psalter of 1340 clearly shows very well-dressed ladies ferreting, although the work probably stylizes the true scene. In his *Livre de Chasse* (circa 1387), Gaston, Comte de Foix, shows drawings of ferreting taking place, complete with a muzzled ferret and several purse-nets. This idea of muzzling ferrets in order to make them unable to kill is one which persists even to today, and yet the practice renders the ferret extremely vulnerable to attacks by rats, which often live in rabbit burrows. Although one can almost forgive 'the ancients' for their ignorance, I find it impossible to forgive modern-day ferreters for this sin. Gaston's work also states that rabbits were only hunted by members of the fur trade.

A fifteenth century Franco-Burgundian tapestry, showing an idealised ferreting scene. Note the purse-nets and dogs. (The Burrell Collection, Glasgow Museum and Art Galleries — The Ferreters' Tapestry)

In 1221, at Termez, a place on the banks of the River Oxus, about 160 miles south of Samarkand (Afghanistan), legend has it that the infamous Genghis Khan used ferrets for hunting rabbits, while in a court roll of 1223, we find the first concrete evidence of ferrets and their use against rabbits in Britain, and there is documentary evidence that a ferreter was attached to the English Royal Court in 1281.

In the thirteenth century, rabbits, and so obviously ferrets, were important to the church and its establishments, as borne out by the many references to ferrets which belonged to quite high ranking churchmen of the time. Rabbits and ferrets were also of great importance to the landed gentry, who did not wish for the peasants to share this bounty. In an attempt to keep ferrets out of the hands of would-be poachers, a law was passed in 1390, which limited the ownership of ferrets to those with a minimum salary of forty shillings per year, the equivalent of a very highly paid executive today. This law indicates that poaching was becoming a major problem, and was obviously designed to exclude ferrets from the lower classes.

The first mention of the white ferret that I can find, is from 1551, in Conrad Gesner's *Historiae Animalum*; this was a book dealing with all quadrupeds, and published in Zürich. The ferret's colour is described by Gesner as 'the colour of wool stained with urine', an excellent description. In 1421, John Lydgate, a Benedictine monk at Bury St Edmunds, England, later prior of Hatfield Broadoak, English poet and friend of Geoffrey Chaucer, wrote the poem *The Seige of Thebes*. One line in this poem mentions the animal's red eyes, another obvious reference to the white ferret.

Queen Elizabeth I, with her 'pet ferret'. The author believes that much of the 'ermine' used to trim the robes of royalty was, in fact, ferret fur —fitch. (The Ermine Portrait of Queen Elizabeth I, by kind permission of the Marquess of Salisbury, The Courtauld Institute of Art)

The lords of the manor in Medieval England thought so highly of the rabbit that they kept specific fields for them to live in, and built warrens to try to ensure that the animals stayed in that area. The men in charge of these artificial warrens were responsible for the protection of the warren and for ensuring that the lord had a regular supply of rabbit meat for his table. These men were referred to as 'warreners', and it is from this that the surname 'Warrener', 'Waren', and 'Warrender' came.

The household books of Lord William Howard of Naworth Castle (1618—1633), make interesting reading, and give us a wonderful insight into life for a warrener. The warrener's house had a tiled roof and a brick floor. He was supplied with a 'wallet' (a carrying bag) for his ferrets, seven yards of coarse cloth for his bed, eight yards of cloth for his blankets, a hank of yarn for mending his nets, a paddle staff with iron on it (an implement for digging out laid-up ferrets etc), various traps — for rabbits and their predators — and a ferret line. In 1622, a ferret room was built for his ferrets (the ferrets were kept in barrels and later hutches in this room, and all of the warrener's ferreting equipment was also stored in the room). Add all this up, along with his not insubstantial wages, and it can be seen that the warrener was a servant of great importance to his master.

Although most people now accept that the rabbit was introduced to Britain by the Normans, some still maintain that it was the Romans. These people argue that the rabbit was used to supplement the soldiers' rations and to ensure that, wherever Rome's Legions marched, there would be food available. The Romans were renowned for taking food animals with them wherever they travelled. One favourite of their senior officers and nobles was the edible dormouse (*Glis glis*); the animals were kept in earthenware jars until they were fat enough for the pot (although I doubt that even then they would provide more than a couple of mouthfuls of meat), and cooked with fruit and nuts before being served. According to Pliny, this practice was banned in 14 BC, because the Roman senators believed that the eating of such delicacies showed too large a degree of ostentatious luxury, and was an affront to the lower classes of Rome; at the same time shellfish and birds were also banned from the tables of the rich citizens of Rome.

The popularity of the ferret in the UK is graphically illustrated by the fact that at the turn of the last century, the British patent office was inundated with applications for registration of patents for ferret cages — a sure indication that the ferret was big business, and expected to get bigger! Their main use at this time was for rodent extermination — a practice that was then also very popular in the United States. According to US sources, tens of thousands of ferrets were raised and sold for this purpose every year at the turn of the twentieth century. The term 'ferretmeister' was used in America, and the Department of Agriculture issued regular bulletins detailing — and encouraging — the ferret's use in rodent abatement.

Throughout its time with man, we have found many uses for the humble ferret. It has been used for hunting; in laboratories for influenza and cold research; fur (the ferret's pelt is known as 'fitch'); as pets, as a fancy animal (ie for exhibition purposes), for ferret racing, and even in industry. The television cables at the Prince of Wales' wedding were put into position by using a ferret; the animal was equipped with a harness, onto which was attached a light but very strong line. The ferret was then sent through the small pipes etc and, when it emerged at the other end, the line was attached to the TV cables, which were then hauled through. This practice is widely used in industry for cables, telephone wires etc.

Legends abound about other uses for the ferret; some claim that it is/was used in the United States space programme, while others claim that the customs and excise authorities in several countries are training the animal to detect drugs, and that the armed forces, police and security forces are training the ferret to detect explosives.

'Camel hair' brushes are made from ferret hair and *not* that of the camel, which in any case is woolly. A 'putois' is a French brush made from ferret hair and used for painting glaze on ceramics.

The Ferret in the United States of America

The ferret was probably taken to America (now the USA) by the first English settlers in the sixteenth and seventeenth centuries, and the animal has since had mixed fortunes in the 'New World'.

In the United States, it is illegal to hunt rabbits with ferrets, although in some states it is permissible to hunt rats with ferrets, providing one has the relevant licence. On the whole, US ferrets are kept as pets, and cost about twenty-five times as much in the US than they do in the UK! Consequently, veterinary surgeons in the US see ferrets far more often than do their British counterparts, although the American Veterinary Medical Association Council on Public Health and Regulatory Veterinary Medicine formally discourages the ownership of pet ferrets. As can be imagined, this has led to much controversy in the veterinary profession, all hinging on whether the ferret is a wild or a domesticated animal. Those against the keeping of pet ferrets argue that it is a wild animal, while those in favour argue that, since the ferret has been domesticated for over 2,000 years, it cannot possibly be considered to be a wild animal.

After the First World War, the ferret was used extensively in rodent control throughout the United States, and the US Department of Agriculture published regular bulletins on all aspects of this work. The widespread availability of effective rodenticides led to the demise of the ferret in professional rodent clearing operations, both in the US and in Great Britain.

Even before this time, ferrets were used for rodent extermination, and an excellent example of this is the Massachusetts Colonial Navy. This was America's Revolutionary War naval militia, and was formed on 29 December 1775, and reactivated in 1967, by an act of the Commonwealth of Massachusetts state legislature, to carry on the traditions of the unit. Ferrets were used on board the 18th Century ships to keep the rat and mouse populations on board under control, and this was recognised at a ceremony at Bristol Community College (USA) on 14 September 1986, when the ferret was officially proclaimed as the mascot of the Colonial Navy of Massachusetts. The first ferret with the title had the pet name 'Pokey', and it is possible to purchase cuddly Pokey toys!

Today, the ferret is looked on very differently in the US, and American ferret owners spend large amounts of money on ferret requisites — food, toys, shampoos etc, and there are even companies who solely produce and/or sell goods for ferrets and their keepers. Many British ferret keepers would love to have the luxury of being able to buy a complete, balanced diet food for their ferrets from a pet shop, or even a supermarket, as their American counterparts can. Unfortunately, I think it will be many years before this is available outside of America.

However, not all US citizens are happy with ferrets as pets, and after a couple of nasty accidents involving ferrets 'attacking' children, several states and organisations are campaigning to have the animals banned, or labelled as a 'wild animal', which would also effectively ban the general public from keeping ferrets as pets. These moves are continuing as this book goes to print.

Historically, the ferret has been categorised as a wild animal in every state except Alaska and West Virginia, and this has limited the habit of keeping these animals as pets. In some states, such as New York, special permits are required, while in California, the only ferrets that can be kept as pets are hobbles (neutered males). Georgia, Massachusetts, New Hampshire and South Carolina have already banned ferrets as pets, citing one reason as the lack of a suitable rabies vaccine for ferrets. The United States Humane Society lists the ferret as an 'exotic animal', and as such actively and publicly discourages the keeping of them as pets. The Society is reputed to be drafting reports to be submitted to forty-six states, in the hope of getting the ferret banned as a pet.

Because of attacks on children (there appear to be very few of these, but the ferret's opponents use them to their own advantage), some areas, including Carson City, Nevada, have banned the sale of ferrets to any household containing a child of three years of age or less. Despite the fact that under US legislation the ferret is now categorised as a domestic animal, Alaska, a state which had always allowed the keeping of pet ferrets, tried to ban them; a pet owner successfully appealed against this decision. Such appeals have also succeeded in defeating motions in other areas, including Maine and West Virginia.

I am sure that the ferret will be with us for many years, but ferret keepers throughout the world should carefully study the history of the ferret in the US, and in particular the moves taken (and still being taken) by individuals, voluntary organisations, professional organisations and even local and national government bodies to ban the keeping of pet ferrets. It could happen in *your* country tomorrow!

The Ferret and the Fur Trade

As stated earlier, ferrets have been used to hunt rabbits for hundreds of years, and these rabbits would have supplied both meat and skins. The skins were made into many items of clothing and even into bags and footwear.

In the mid-nineteenth century, many people in mainland Europe kept and bred ferrets for their fur, which was called 'fitch'. The practice caught on in the USA in 1900, and there has been considerable interest in fitch fur production ever since in that country. Until the late 1980s, the popularity of fitch fur production was spreading rapidly, with fitch farms in Australia, Canada, the USA, New Zealand and many European countries. However, fashions change, and fitch, along with many other furs, fell out of favour in many countries in the late 1980s, although it would seem that the pendulum has again swung, and fur is once more being seen as acceptable, with some even making the claim that it is a 'green' (ie environmentally friendly) product!

It was (and still is) common practice to hybridize ferrets with European and Steppe polecats, to get better quality and nicer looking fur.

Ferret Legging

This so-called 'sport' involves the placing of ferrets inside one's trousers, and until recently competitions were held to find the 'world champion ferret legger', ie the one who could keep a ferret down his trousers for the longest period of time. Under the rules of the 'championships', all ferrets used must have a full set of teeth, and the human involved could not wear any underwear. Poor ferrets!

Because of the stresses on the ferrets involved, animal welfare organisations have managed to have the 'sport' banned, and the last record holder was a seventy-two-year-old man from Yorkshire, England, who kept a ferret down his trousers for almost five and a half hours.

The origins of this horrendous activity were probably born out of necessity. As a poacher, one would not wish to advertise the fact that one had a ferret about one's person, and so carrying the animal in a bag or a box would be out of the question. Instead, the poacher would have hidden the ferret about his person, possibly down his trouser legs. As it was common practice until very recently to stitch the ferret's lips together, in order to prevent him biting a human or killing a rabbit, the poacher would probably have been in no danger from the animal's teeth, although its claws could still have made injuries.

Another theory is that, after working ferrets in the winter cold, the animal would have been in need of warming, and by placing it inside one's own clothing, this would have been achieved. Personally, I prefer to place my ferret in a weather-proof carry-ing-box, along with a good supply of warm hay!

Biomedical Research

In the 1900s, the ferret's potential as a model for biomedical research was recognised, and it has been — and still is — used for research into a cure for human influenza, a malady that can also badly affect ferrets naturally. Today, the ferret is used as a labo-ratory (research) animal for physiology, virology, immunology, pharmacology, toxi-cology, and teratology.

***

We will probably never really know whether it was the Normans or the Romans who were responsible for the introduction of the rabbit to the United Kingdom, but the introduction was undoubtedly for their use as a source of food. I have no doubt, however, that whoever was responsible for the introduction of the rabbit to Great Britain, was also responsible for the first use of the domesticated polecat or ferret.

I believe that the ferret has been around for a very long time (at least 1,500 years) in various parts of the world, where it has been used to help its owners to catch their food, and I feel equally certain that the ferret will be with us for many more years, and will still be used for hunting quarry such as the rabbit. I believe that the ferret is simply a domesticated form of the European polecat, *Mustela putorius*, although I would like to investigate further the speculation that today's ferret is the product of crosses between Asiatic (*M. eversmanni*) and European (*M. putorius*) polecats.

Scientific Classification of the Ferret

The ferret belongs to the weasel tribe, or *mustelidae* ('seeker of mice', 'those who carry off mice', the name refers to the musty smell), and is thus related to such animals as the otter, badger and the skunk. It is also a carnivore, and thus related to cats (including lions and tigers), dogs (including wolves and foxes) and civets (meerkats and mongooses).

The *Mustelidae* is an extremely diverse family of mammals which includes terres-trial, aquatic and arboreal species. While most are true carnivores, some have evolved very specialised feeding. There are twenty-six genera, sixty-seven species and over 400 subspecies of mustelids recognised by scientists, and no doubt more will be added. They are endemic throughout the world, with the exception of Antarctica, Australia, Madagascar, New Guinea, New Zealand, most of the Philippines, Sulawsi, the West Indies, and most oceanic islands.

Almost without exception, mustelids are renowned for their fur, and many species have suffered due to the fur trade, while many are of great economic significance in some communities; the best illustration of this is the sable (*Martes zibellina*).

There are five subfamilies, viz; *Mustelinae* (weasels), *Mellivorinae* (honey badger or ratel), *Melinae* (badgers), *Mephitinae* (skunks), and the *Lutrinae* (otters). The pelage is either uniformly coloured, striped or spotted, with some species turning white in winter in the northern parts of their range (controlled by photoperiod). In most species, the body is long and slender; however, the wolverine and badgers are stocky. All have short ears, which are either rounded or pointed, and have short limbs with five digits on each. The claws are non-retractable, and are curved and compressed, with the badgers' claws being larger and heavier, as an adaptation for digging. In otters, the digits are usually webbed.

Males of all species in this family have a baculum (a bone in the penis), and most species have well developed anal scent glands. Skulls are sturdy, with short facial regions, and the dental formula is;

(i 3/2 — 3, c 1/1, pm 2 — 4/2 — 4 , m 1/1 — 2) x 2 = 28 — 38

Enhydra is the sole genus with two lower incisors.

All mustelids are either nocturnal or diurnal, sheltering in trees, burrows or crevices, while badgers usually dig elaborate burrows, known as setts or cettes. The smaller, slender forms in this family move with a characteristic wave-like motion and, when excited, will bounce with stiff legs. The larger members of the family move with a rolling bear-like shuffle.

Mustelids are carnivorous (otters eat mainly aquatic animals), although some species occasionally feed on plant material, while a few are omnivorous. All have highly developed hearing and sight, but tend to hunt by scent, and many species, including *Mustella*, *Poecilogale*, *Gulo*, and certain badgers, are storers of food. Many mustelids have anal glands capable of exuding a fetid secretion when threatened or attacked.

Delayed implantation occurs in many species of this family; although gestation is about thirty-five to sixty-five days, in *Lutra canadensis*, pregnancy can last as long as twelve months.

There is usually a single litter each year, although some species will produce a second litter if mated early in the summer. Offspring are self sufficient at about eight weeks, sexually mature between one to two years, and can live from five to twenty-five years.

Classification of the Mustelidae

ORDER..............................**Carnivora** — 7 families, 93 genera, 231 species.
This order includes cats (including lions and tigers), dogs (including foxes, jackals and wolves), bears (including polar and grizzly), raccoons (including coatis and giant pandas), weasels (including stoats and polecats), civets (including meerkats and mongooses) and hyenas.

FAMILY..............................**Mustelidae** — 26 genera, 67 species.
The *mustelidae* are to be found all over the world, in every continent except Australia and Antarctica. Their habitat ranges from arctic tundra to tropical rain-forest on land, in trees, in rivers and in the ocean.

Animals in this tribe range in size from the diminutive least weasel (*Mustella nivalis rixosa*), which measures fifteen centimetres head to tail with a tail length of three to four centimetres and weighing as little as thirty grams and is the smallest carnivore known to man, to the massive bulk of the grison (*Galictis vittata*), a mammal from Central and South America, which resembles a wolverine and can attain sizes of up to 120 centimetres head to tail with a tail of up to sixty-five centimetres and weighing up to thirty kilograms. One of the most recently described sub-species of the *Mustelidae*, is the Hainan small-toothed ferret-badger (*Melogale moschata hainanensis*).

SUB-FAMILY..........................**Mustelinae** — 10 genera, 34 species.
These include the grisons, martens, mink, polecats and weasels. They are terrestrial hunters of small vertebrates, although some (particularly the martens) are excellent climbers.

Members of the Sub-Family **Mustelinae**

M. africana	Tropical weasel
M. altaica	Mountain weasel
M. ermininea	Common stoat (ermine)
M. eversmanni	Steppe polecat
M. felipei	Columbian weasel
M. frenata	Long-tailed weasel
M. kathiah	Yellow-bellied weasel
M. lutreola	European mink
M. lutreolina	Indonesian mountain weasel
M. nigripes	Black-footed ferret
M. nivalis	European common weasel
M. nivalis rixosa	Least weasel
M. nudipes	Malaysian weasel
M. putorius	European polecat
M. putorius furo	Domesticated ferret
M. sibirica	Siberian weasel
M. strigidorsa	Back-striped weasel
M. vison	American mink
Vormela peregusna	Marbled polecat
Martes americana	American marten
M. flavigula	Yellow-throated marten
M. foina	Beech marten
M. martes	Pine marten
M. melampus	Japanese marten
M. pennanti	Fisher
M. zibellina	Sable
Eira barbata	Tayra
Galictis cuja	Little grison
G. vittata	Greater grison
Lyncodon patagonicus	Patagonian weasel
Ictonyx striatus	Zorilla, or striped polecat
Poecilictis libyca	Saharan striped weasel
Poecilogale albinucha	White-naped weasel
Gulo	Wolverine

The Black-footed ferret

The black-footed ferret was once extremely common on the Great Plains in the United States, with the estimated population in 1920 being 500,000. However, throughout the twentieth century, they have suffered as a result of the extermination — mainly by humans, but also by disease — of its sole prey, the prairie dog (*Cynomys spp*). The animals gradually became a rarity, and excitement spread among zoologists with the discovery of a small population in South Dakota, in 1964. Some of these ferrets were captured and taken into captivity, but no breeding took place. In 1974, all traces of this population vanished, and it was assumed by many that the black-footed ferret had passed into the oblivion that is extinction.

Then, on 26 September 1981, dogs on a ranch near Meeteetse, Wyoming, killed a ferret, and the rancher's wife was so impressed by the cadaver, that he took it to a taxidermist for mounting. Luckily, the taxidermist correctly identified the animal, and US Fish and Wildlife Service agents were alerted to the presence of what was to turn out to be a very large (possibly the largest ever observed) colony of black-footed ferrets. The agents succeed in trapping a ferret, which was fitted with a radio transmitter collar, and then released, and tracked it until it led the agents to the colony. After intensive field studies of the area by scientists, the population was estimated at 129 animals in 1984.

The excitement and elation of the discovery was short-lived, however, as the number of ferrets rapidly declined in 1985, as the result of a plague in their prey species, the white-tailed prairie dog (*Cynomys leucurus*). As feverish efforts were made to control the plague in the prairie dogs, canine distemper was accidentally introduced into the population of black-footed ferrets (probably by the dog of one of the field workers), and this had a disastrous effect; by 1986, only 18 ferrets remained — the last of their species.

Scientists made a controversial decision, and captured all of the animals, placing them in captivity. Never before had such a drastic step been taken to help prevent an animal becoming extinct, but the need was great. Scientists worked hard, and finally managed to get the animals to breed, the first litter being fathered by a male known as 'Scarface'. Scarface went on to father many more litters before his death on 15 June 1992, and this fact caused many problems, as scientists tried to ensure that inbreeding depression did not occur.

By August 1992, there were over 240 black-footed ferrets in captivity, and a release programme has been initiated, releasing selected animals back into the wild. Two areas have been chosen, both in Wyoming; the Shirley Basin/Medicine Bow area, and the Meeteetse area. Scientists have appealed to humans to avoid shooting prairie dogs and not to disturb the black-footed ferrets. They have also asked that any dogs taken to the area should be fully vaccinated against distemper.

The ferret release sites are very small (about 1,500 acres), and it is to be hoped that humans can be persuaded to give this magnificent animal the opportunity to recolonise the area — an opportunity it so richly deserves.

The black-footed ferret is the most endangered mammal in the USA, and is the only member of the weasel tribe currently listed as 'Endangered' by the International Union for the Conservation of Nature (IUCN); it is similarly listed by the USDI, and is on Appendix 1 of the Convention on International Trade in Endangered Species.

The rarest ferrets in the world!
The American black-footed ferret was
thought to be extinct, and would have
been had it not been for the intensive
captive breeding programme.
(Photos courtesy of the Wyoming Game
and Fish Department)

Mustelid Characteristics

The reproductive habits and characteristics of *mustelids* deserve some mention here. For most of the time, the sexes keep themselves to themselves and, when they do meet, they are often extremely hostile towards one another. It is only when the female is in oestrus (on heat) that a (temporary) truce is called. Then the male takes hold of the female by the scruff of the neck, often almost brutally, and then proceeds to drag her around until he finds a suitable 'honeymoon site', where he then mounts her.

Copulation is prolonged and repeated (it can last for over two hours) and this is facilitated by the baculum of the male (a bone in the penis). The mating often seems to be almost a fight between the male and female. This is probably nature's way of ensuring that only the strongest pass on their characteristics to the next generation since, if the male cannot 'overpower' the female, he will not be able to mate her.

In some mustelids, delayed implantation occurs. This is where the fertilised egg simply floats around in the uterus until being implanted in the uterus wall at a later date. This date can be anything from a few days to almost one year! (This is not the case with the ferret).

The Attraction of the Ferret

Ferrets are intelligent and clean; even though they do have a characteristic smell, they have excellent habits, always using the same area for defecating and urinating. They keep their fur meticulously clean, spending long hours grooming themselves. They are also entertaining to watch as they go through their everyday antics. Watching a ferret trying to break an egg will keep anyone enthralled for hours; I often wonder, at the risk of sounding anthropomorphic, if the ferret really *is* trying to break the egg, or simply playing with it first, before he decides to eat it!

Since 1982, I have spent much of the summer months travelling around the UK to various events with my 'Ferret Roadshow', putting on displays with my ferrets. At these events, it is common for the public to ask about the ferrets' reputed 'viciousness'. At these — and many other times — several ferrets were lifted from their cages and offered to members of the perpetual crowd which always gathers around such displays. As all of my ferrets are regularly handled from a very early age (some even from birth), I had no worries.

On one such occasion I placed Izzy, my favourite jill, on the top of the display while I gave a talk on the merits of the ferret (I never need an excuse for this!). While I was talking, a young girl began blowing in Izzy's face and generally tormenting her. Izzy bristled and began making warning noises. I saw what was happening and interrupted my talk to ask the girl not to torment the ferrets, and then I continued with my talk. A few minutes later, Izzy was again warning the girl and I again warned her myself, as did the girl's mother. To no avail; the girl continued her tormenting and I was just about to tell the girl again, when Izzy decided that she had had enough. She uttered a loud 'chatter' and, turning around, ran across the top of the display and wormed her way into my coat pocket — her favourite travelling area and one where she knew that she would not be bothered by ill-mannered humans! Izzy, even during extreme provocation, had been the perfect lady that I always knew she was!

Ferreting is not solely a male domain; many ladies, too, love the sport.

Some ferrets love to travel in their owner's pocket! This is Izzy, a jill which lived almost fourteen years, in the pocket of the author's wife, Jane.

In normal use, a little musk is passed out with the animal's faeces, thus effectively marking the area for all of the other individuals in the vicinity. Some pet owners do not like the idea of their ferrets ever having a chance of discharging this obnoxious smelling fluid in the home, and have their veterinary surgeon remove the anal gland. This is a very controversial subject, and many vets will refuse to carry out the operation on ethical grounds. It should always be remembered that the ferret's musky odour is produced by skin secretions, with the hob's stronger smelling urine as a contributory factor to the animal's smell, and the removal of the anal glands will not reduce these sources of odour. 'Descenting' is a mutation, and I would not recommend owners to have their pets operated on in this manner. Often, a result of such an operation is impairment of the function of the animal's anal sphincter muscle, leading to various degrees of incontinence.

Removal of the anal gland may, however, be necessary on medical grounds, and owners should be guided on this matter by their own veterinary surgeon.

***

In conclusion, I would state that the ferret is a wonderful, intelligent animal. It is eminently suitable as either a pet or a working animal and can — indeed often does — fulfil both roles at the same time. Ferrets deserve better care, and it is the intent of this book to ensure that they get this.

Chapter 2

Selection

Properly cared for — housing, diet, handling, health care etc — ferrets can live for up to fourteen years, and so the choice of suitable ferrets must be given considerable thought. Indeed, much thought must be given to whether or not you are a suitable person to keep ferrets. You may consider this remark to be facetious, but I assure you that those running ferret rescue centres will not; it is a sad fact that all too many people take on the responsibility of keeping animals with little thought, and this leads to many thousands of animals being abandoned. I know of one UK-based ferret rescue society where the secretary has had over a hundred rescued ferrets in his keeping at one time, and so I urge everyone to remember that if you decide to buy a ferret today, it is going to be with you for a long time. A fifteen-year-old may not want to take his pet with him when he becomes a married man of twenty-four, but the ferret may still have almost a third of its life to live.

Ferret kits have plenty of 'Ahh' appeal, and may encourage the purchase of such an animal on a whim, when the prospective owner has no idea of the animal's requirements, and will not even have a suitable cage for the kit on its arrival home. Such purchases must be avoided — for everyone's sake.

The fact that you are taking the time and trouble to read this book indicates to me that you recognise the qualities that ferrets and their relatives possess. If you are reading this book before purchasing your ferrets, you will avoid most — if not all — of the potential problems associated with keeping these highly intelligent animals. If you already have your ferrets — perhaps have been keeping and breeding ferrets for a few years — but still choose to read this or any other book on the subject, this tells me that you really do have the well-being of your ferrets at heart. You obviously wish to ensure that you keep up-to-date with developments in ferret husbandry, and also to see how other people look at the subject. I truly believe that no-one will ever know all there is to know about ferrets, and that we can all learn from other's experiences.

Once you have given a great deal of thought as to whether or not to proceed with your decision to acquire a ferret, and you are certain that you can give the animal a real home for all of its life, there are certain other questions which you will want answering. These include:

> Where and when will you purchase your ferret(s)?
> What should you look for to indicate a sound, healthy ferret?
> What should you avoid in your purchase?
> How many ferrets should you keep and should they all be obtained at the same time and from the same person?
> Which sex makes the best pet or working ferret?
> How do you differentiate between the sexes?
> How do you assess the character of your intended purchases?
> What colour(s) should you choose?
> What is the best size ferret to purchase?
> At what age should your ferrets be obtained?

Let us examine all of these questions.

Where and When to Purchase Your Ferret(s)

All jills (ie female ferrets) come into season in early spring, when the days begin to get longer, and the nights shorter. In the UK, this is in March, but in other parts of the world, it will be a different month. However, some commercial breeders will alter the ferrets' photoperiod, thereby enabling the animals to breed all year round (see chapter 6, 'Breeding' for more details). Because of this phenomena of photoperiodism, young ferrets are normally only available at certain times of the year, ie summer; this then, is the best time to buy your ferrets.

At other times of the year, you may well see ferrets being advertised for sale, but unless they are bred by someone who has tweaked the animal's photoperiod, they will obviously not be kits, ie they will be over sixteen weeks of age. All too often, the reason for the ferrets appearing on the market is because they have proved less than suitable for their current owners. It may be that the animal has grown too big, or has not been handled properly and is therefore rather inclined to bite, or simply not tamed. If it is a working ferret, it may have developed some bad habits, such as skulking (see chapter 4, for more information on this point). In other words, these ferrets are usually someone's rejects, and there is always a reason for that rejection. I always advise people to leave these animals alone, although I am aware that some — a very small minority in my experience — are being sold for bona fide reasons, and will make good purchases. It is far better to await the sale of kits, ie ferrets under sixteen weeks, although this may necessitate waiting for some months. It is worth bearing in mind the maxim 'He who acts in haste, repents at his leisure'!

Ferrets are sold by many people, from the person who gives loving care to his ferrets, and simply breeds one or two litters a year to ensure continuation of his line, to commercial breeders who have many hundreds of ferrets kept and bred in order to make money for their owners. In between these two extremes are many others, who include good and bad ferret keepers, all with their own reasons for breeding and selling the animals.

Wherever possible, go to an established ferret breeder who has a proven reputation, and who has been keeping and breeding ferrets for several years. While no such person will let you have their very best ferrets — they will want to keep those for their own purposes — neither will they risk a hard-earned reputation by selling you inferior stock.

In some countries, the only purveyors of ferrets are pet shops; as with breeders, there are good ones and bad ones, and you should take great care to choose the pet shops with which you deal.

When buying a ferret, try to visit the breeder's home or base of operations, and look carefully at the parents of the kits being offered for sale, along with all other ferrets and/or other animals kept by the seller. All cages should be clean, of an adequate size, and not overcrowded. Look at the latrine corner; the faeces should be hard, dark brown, and have only a slight smell. Examine all of the adults; are they tame? If not, then the breeder probably has not handled them enough, and may simply be keeping them for breeding to make money.

Are they all in good condition? What are they being fed on? Many people feed their ferrets on totally unsuitable diets (see chapter 5, for more information on adequate diets), and so the offspring of these malnourished animals may well be suffering because of this.

In the UK, it is a regular sight at the many country fairs, held all over the country throughout the summer months, to see individuals walking around the showground with boxes of ferret kits for sale. These people do not have the interests of their ferrets at heart, merely wanting to get rid of the kits to save having to look after and feed them. If they were caring owners they would not have bred excess kits in the first place.

Never be tempted to buy a ferret from someone like this; you have never seen them before, and it is certain that you will never see them again. You have no idea of the conditions under which they have been bred, and to buy from such people merely creates a market. Many people do buy such ferrets, but many are sold to children or those who have not really thought through the pros and cons of keeping ferrets. Many of the purchasers will not have a suitable cage for their new pets, and many will change their minds before reaching home, abandoning the ferrets by the roadside — a cruel, callous and illegal act.

What to Look For and What to Avoid

A healthy ferret will have energy and a *joie de vivre*, bouncing around in his cage, and playing with his siblings. His eyes will be bright, ears held erect, coat shiny and clean, and his motions will be hard and have only a slight smell. An ill ferret will be entirely different; he will be lethargic, lying down and sleeping for most of the day. His ears will be flat against his head, his coat matted and dirty, staring and greasy to the touch; he may have a discharge from his eyes, ears, sex opening or anus, and he may also have diarrhoea.

Under no circumstances should you buy any ferret from a cage containing one or more ferrets as described at the end of the last paragraph; to do so would be foolish. Even if the ferret which you purchase is not exhibiting the symptoms, he is almost certain to be infected and, if you place him with others, he will pass on this ailment to all the ferrets with which he comes into contact.

How Many Ferrets Should Be Kept?

There are conflicting thoughts on how many ferrets should be kept together. Some people hark back to the ferret's wild ancestor, and point out that the polecat is a solitary creature, and so the ferret is best kept on its own.

I personally believe that ferrets are happier when kept in groups (known as a 'business'). My own ferrets are kept in communal cages where I can have up to fifteen ferrets all living happily together, although this may change during the breeding season (see chapter 6).

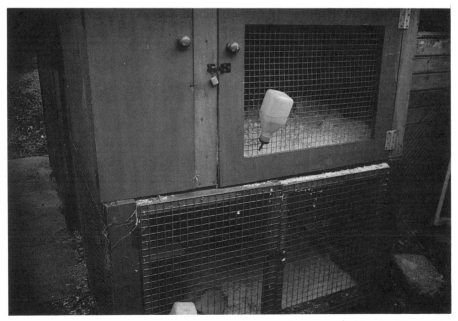

A two-tier ferret court. The bottom and top can be connected by flexible, corrugated drainage pipe, allowing the ferrets access to both levels, or without, as separate cubs.

I really do feel that a single ferret, kept on its own all of its life, will not be as happy as it would if it had access to a fellow ferret.

Initially, I recommend that two jills are kept, as ferrets like company of their own kind and two hobs, unless kept together from a very early age may fight, especially during the breeding season. A hob and a jill kept together will inevitably produce young, bringing with them the problems of space, food and handling. A couple of years' experience are needed before breeding should be embarked on.

If you are intending to hunt with your ferrets, but not to use one of the many electronic ferret detectors that are on the market, a 'liner' is essential. This is a large hob who is kept on his own and, in the event of a lay-up, is sent into the burrow attached to a long line (hence the name) to find the dead rabbit, move the errant free-working ferret and then curl up next to the dead rabbit. You then dig along the line (which is marked every metre or so) until you find the liner and rabbit (easier said than done). The liner must, of course, be big and strong enough to pull the line through all of the tunnels and then frighten away the free working ferret. (See chapter 7).

With the advent of good quality, efficient and relatively cheap electronic 'ferret detectors', liners have almost become a thing of the past, with more and more people turning to the new technology and ignoring the old ways. While this is, in itself, not a bad thing, it should also be remembered that even high technology equipment can break down. When this happens, it is usually at a time when it is far from convenient. At such times, it is reassuring to know that you have more than one string to your bow. The possession of, and experience with, a good liner will often prove to be of incalculable benefit to those who regularly work their ferrets. I would always recommend any newcomer to the sport to use a liner for at least two seasons of regular work before trying an electronic detector.

The modern equivalent of a liner, is the use of a hob with anti-social tendencies towards other ferrets (as with the original liners), but, instead of using a line, he wears an electronic collar. Other than this one difference, his use is the same as a liner on a line.

I must admit that since I first tried one of these marvellous inventions, I have never worked my ferrets without one. Ferret detectors are discussed fully in chapter 7.

Should the Ferrets Be Obtained At the Same Time and From the Same Source?

Some ferrets will not readily accept other ferrets, although my own experience shows that, provided the introduction is made when all of the animals concerned are young, and just after they have had a full feed (with all of the excess food removed from the cage), this is not usually a problem. True, when first introduced, the ferrets will probably have a very noisy 'fight', but this is simply to establish the hierarchy or pecking order, and usually lasts for no more than a few minutes, with no major injuries to either party. It is, however, worth checking the ferrets for wounds, and treating them accordingly, within a few hours of the fight.

If you are intending to breed from your ferrets, there are good reasons to ensure that the ferrets are not related, while it could easily be argued that there are good reasons to ensure that the ferrets are related; see chapter 10 for more details.

Related ferrets will almost certainly share similar characteristics, while totally unrelated ferrets may give birth to kits which seem to resemble neither parent!

Which Sex Makes the Best Pet or Working Ferret?

Both sexes make good working animals and/or pets, but they also both have their problems, and it is worth considering these before deciding which sex to choose.

The jill (female ferret) will normally come into season (oestrus) in the spring each year and, unless mated, will stay in season until the winter, ie about six months. During this time, she will be unpredictable, bad tempered and generally difficult to live with, qualities shared by most female mammals when they are in oestrus! It is from this characteristic, exhibited noticeably in the female dog, that we get the derogatory term 'bitch'.

A jill's vulva will swell and protrude from her body by up to two centimetres, causing it to trail on the ground, and allowing ingress of dirt and grime — potentially harmful to her. All the while she is in season, the female sex hormone, oestrogen, will be present in her body in large amounts, and this too can prove dangerous (see chapter 6 for more details), usually leading, over a number of years, to leukaemia and thence death, if she is allowed to stay in oestrus.

Hobs (male ferrets) often become quite aggressive with other ferrets in the breeding season (although this aggression should not extend to human handlers, provided that the handling is done with care), repeatedly mating — or at least attempting to — any females in their cage, regardless of their state of oestrus, and fighting with other males. I always recommend, therefore, that all hobs are housed separately in the summer months, in order to reduce the risks of injuries to them and other ferrets housed with them. At the very minimum, a spare cage for every hob should be available for use as and when required.

If you are certain that you will never wish to breed with your ferrets, then you should have them neutered (jills spayed and hobs castrated). If this is done, then these animals can usually live happily together throughout the year, regardless of their gender. A word of warning about castration; it is not the panacea for aggression and 'male problems' that some would have you believe, and it also carries with it certain possible medical problems (see chapter 9 for more details).

If you feel that you do not wish to have a litter from your jills, then they should either be mated with a vasectomized hob (a hoblet), or given drugs to take them out of oestrus (see chapter 6 for more details). Anyone who intends to take the hobby of ferret keeping seriously should have a hoblet of their own, as this is, to my mind, the simplest and most straightforward method of removing jills from oestrus and, apart from the possibility of a pseudo pregnancy, has no deleterious side-effects. Even the short-term effects of a pseudo pregnancy can easily be overcome (see chapter 6).

How Do You Differentiate Between the Sexes?

The sexing of ferrets is simplicity itself, even in very young animals. In the jill, the vaginal opening and the anus are very close together, whereas in the hob, the penal opening and the anus are far apart. Do not make the mistake of thinking that the

A jill (left) and a hob, showing sexual dimorphism.

hob will have two easily visible testicles, since these do not descend until the breeding season after the birth of the hob and, even in adult hobs, they are drawn back up into the body in cold weather. Likewise, it is highly unlikely that the male's penis will be seen, as it is usually kept inside the body cavity, except during mating.

34

How to Assess the Character of Your Intended Purchases

By carefully looking at and examining the parents of your intended purchases, you should gain a great insight into the characters of their offspring. Fierce, aggressive and 'untamed' parents will almost certainly produce difficult to handle kits, while 'quiet' ferrets (ie those which are very tame, and easily handleable) will also pass on these traits to their progeny. It is, of course, possible to tame almost any animal, but it is easier (and a lot less painful) to begin with kits from quiet parents.

When making your choice from a litter of ferrets, do not choose the ones which rush at your fingers and snap at you; these animals may turn out to be too aggressive or difficult to handle and control.

Neither should you choose the ones which hide in the background or are too frightened to come out of their nest-box, as fear can also lead to aggression. The best kits will be those who are cautious but inquisitive. Try to tempt these animals to come to you by gently talking to them, or offering small pieces of meat. When they are at your hands, do not try to lift them, but merely stroke them; if they allow this to happen, even if it takes a couple of minutes, then gently pick them up. If they are unconcerned by your attentions, but inquisitive about your smell or their surroundings, and do not struggle unduly, these kits will probably grow into excellent ferrets.

Well handled and cared for ferrets are not sly, devious or untrustworthy; neither do they bite without good reason. Since 1982, I have travelled around the UK with my Ferret Roadshow. During this time, literally thousands of people have handled my ferrets — some none too gently! Not one finger has ever been nipped — let alone bitten — during that time. This is indisputable proof — if proof be needed — that there is no such thing as a nasty ferret, only misguided and thoughtless owners.

We are all rather vain creatures, and all appreciate the opportunity to sing our own praises. If you like the ferrets that you see, tell the owner. He will undoubtedly be more than pleased at such remarks, often visibly swelling with pride! Such a compliment is worth more than gold to a true ferreter.

When it comes to time to discuss the cost, you may find that the breeder will ask only a very small sum, perhaps with the condition that, should he be so inclined, he can come to you in future years for some stock, again at a reasonable price. On the other hand, you may get a nasty surprise when the breeder asks you for several times the price that you had in mind. Do not be put off! I often use this ploy to see just how keen and committed any potential buyers are, before I will part with my precious stock. I also use the same ploy to rid myself of time wasters and people who I just do not feel would make suitable owners for my ferrets!

When you have chosen your ferret(s), take them home and place them in their previously prepared cage, complete with water and food. Remember that these youngsters will have been used to the company and play of their siblings and, when they suddenly find themselves without this, they may be rather unsettled. For this reason, it is advisable to spend time playing with and handling them. This will also set the scene for a healthy rapport in the future.

What Colour(s) Should You Choose?

To me, the colour of a ferret is immaterial; I want a ferret with the right characteristics for their job and for ease of handling. I have kept almost every possible colour of ferret and the one thing that I have learned is that the colour of an animal's coat does not give any guarantees about the way the animal behaves. Almost without exception, when a ferret does not behave properly, it is as a direct result of its human handler. Choose the ferret which most appeals to you!

People will give conflicting views on what makes a 'good ferret'; some will tell you that all white ferrets are susceptible to illnesses and are generally too weak. Others will say that 'poleys' (naturally coloured ferrets) are too wild and will never be completely tame. You will hear the often quoted (but still not true) view that only white ferrets should be worked, as their dark coloured relations cannot be easily seen when out working in dense cover. Equally, some people will tell you that, as most ferreting takes place in the winter months, when there is very often snow on the ground, only dark ferrets should be used, as white ferrets will not show up! As it is necessary for all of one's senses to be finely tuned and alert to all that is happening during any hunting trip, failure to see a ferret exit from a burrow should not be blamed on the ferret's colour.

I have kept albinos, polecats and almost every colour in-between. They have all worked as well as I have allowed them to and the only one to make any mistakes has been me.

I like to see some variety in my stock and, providing that the ferret is a good worker, colour is completely immaterial to me. It is possible to breed ferrets of a particular colour, eg all polecats, all white, some of each and perhaps some colours which are neither one nor the other. To do this, one needs to have a working knowledge of simple Mendelian genetics and to know the breeding and parentage (for at least three generations) of all one's ferrets. Even with all of this knowledge, the actual results may never be exactly as they were worked out on paper! Full details of the genetical aspects of selective colour breeding are to be found in chapter 10.

What is the Best Size Ferret to Purchase?

Size is another contentious area; some favour giant ferrets while others go for tiny 'greyhound' types. There are pros and cons to every school of thought and, if you are to remain happy with your original choice — and their future progeny — it is best that all schools of thought are examined thoroughly.

Always bear in mind that the hob will be much bigger than the jill (up to two and a half times bigger). Hobs vary in size from about one to two kilograms or even two and a half kilograms, while jills can weigh as little as four hundred grams. Apart from this 'sexual dimorphism', if you are keeping the ferret for a pet, size is not really important. However, if you are keeping a ferret for working, then size is an important factor, as it is possible to have a ferret that is too big for work (see chapter 7 for more details).

Due to their larger size, hobs tend to be worked less often than jills; this is not to say that they cannot be worked, as I have successfully used many hobs over the years. I feel that it may well be due to the fact that the male does not produce young and, as many ferreters wish to see fresh stock every year, few bother to keep hobs. When the time comes for their jills to be mated, the owners simply borrow a hob from a friend. While this can be advantageous, it can also be dangerous in that, without one's own hob(s), it is almost impossible to develop a 'line' (as described in chapter 10), the result being that litters vary in size, number of young, character and many other features. If you do decide to rely upon other owners' hobs, ensure that you check the quality and nature of the hob *before* you decide to use it; this will help ensure that you breed the type of ferret that you really want.

Ferrets come in a wide variety of shapes and sizes, all with their own adherents and champions. The arguments put forward to support each are numerous; large ferrets have more stamina (they also have more weight to carry), small ferrets are faster (but have less stamina), large ferrets are easier to see and can drag rabbits out of stops (dead ends), small ferrets can climb over such rabbits and thus flush them out of the stop. I have tried most types and am a great believer that small ferrets make the best workers. The ferrets should not be so small that they tire within five minutes of being put into a hole, but neither should they be so large that they cannot easily pass through the mesh of an average purse-net without disturbing it unduly.

These smaller ferrets seem to have the ability to be able to climb over the backs of rabbits which have set themselves into a stop, with their nose against the wall and back feet kicking out viciously. This ability results in fewer lay-ups (ie killed rabbits which are then eaten by the ferret, who then decides to take forty winks). Larger ferrets will simply scratch and eat away at the back of the rabbit, until the animal is dead. This almost always results in lost meat — a waste! — and digging.

A legend has grown up around a very small strain of ferret, known as 'greyhound ferrets'. These ferrets are very tiny — never more than about fifteen to twenty centimetres long, and weighing less than four hundred grams — and extremely quick in their movements. They are said to have the ability to *always* flush rabbits out of stops and can also take on, out manoeuvre and then kill any rat — no matter what size — that they encounter. I have met many people who are trying to breed such animals; I have also met some people who claim to own such animals. However, I have never actually met any of these ferrets! I am not saying that they have not existed in the past, nor that they do not exist today, just that I have never actually encountered any of these 'super ferrets'. Every sport and hobby has its own legends and tales of outstanding characters and events, and I wonder if these too-good-to-be-true ferrets are not perhaps just a figment of imagination, rather like the massive fish that always eludes capture by the angler and, somehow, always seems to get bigger with every telling of the story?

At What Age Should Your Ferrets Be Obtained?

As stated earlier, I recommend that kits of between the age of eight to sixteen weeks are obtained. Both younger and older animals are often offered for sale, but animals less than eight weeks should never be purchased, as they are not mature enough to leave their mother; like many animals, ferret kits learn much from their mother by observing her natural behaviour. Play and other activities with siblings is equally important to a kit's development.

When older animals are offered for sale, there is a good reason, and it is usually because the current owner has mistreated the animal, or the ferret has acquired bad habits. Treat with the utmost suspicion anyone trying to sell adult ferrets — even if they have a plausible excuse!

What Makes a Good Ferret?

Everyone has their own ideas on this subject, and very few will agree on all aspects. To me, a good ferret is one which performs its tasks well — be it a hunter or a pet — and is easy to handle, come what may. I do not like ferrets which bite, although I do realise that this trait is probably the fault of the breeder/owner rather than the ferret.

Some ferrets appeal to me because of their looks, ie they are aesthetically pleasing *to me*, but remember the old saying 'Beauty is in the eyes of the beholder', and different looks appeal to different people. If *you* like the looks of a particular ferret, and the way that it behaves — its nature and behaviour — then that ferret will be a good ferret for you. If there is one aspect of the ferret that you don't like — be it size, colour, or nature — then it is a bad ferret *for you*!

Handling and Taming

Good ferrets do not bite and, to my mind, there is no such thing as a bad ferret, simply too many bad owners of ferrets. From an early age, ferret kits must be handled gently but carefully; with this type of treatment they will soon learn that your hands are wonderful, but definitely not on the menu! They will come to trust you, and look forward to your handling them. Never, during all of the time that I have been involved with ferrets, have I been seriously bitten by one of my own ferrets. On the few occasions that a ferret has nipped me, it has always been due to my own clumsiness.

I know all of my ferrets well, and they trust me implicitly. Because of this, I can handle my young stock while they are still in the nest. At this age I expect to have my fingers nibbled by the kits but, as they are so young and weak, this is not a painful experience. Nevertheless, the youngsters need to be taught that your fingers are not on the menu, and I do this by gently tapping their noses every time that they try to bite me. They soon learn.

Throughout the time that I am handling them, I keep up a constant conversation with them, in a soft and soothing tone of voice. I believe that the voice is just as important as the hands, and can be used to calm and reassure ferrets of any age; this habit of talking to small, furry animals does, however, give rise to strange looks from non-animal people!

The next step is for me to dip my fingers into a mixture of milk and egg, offering my fingers to the youngsters to lick. If they try to bite me, they receive a gentle tap on the side of their nose; within a very short time, the kits are entirely trustworthy.

It is important to keep all movements steady and smooth; if you make sudden, unexpected movements, the ferrets may nip through fear. If that happens, it is not fair to blame the ferret.

When picking up ferrets, place one hand around their torso, with the thumb and first finger around the neck and the other hand under its backside, to take the animal's weight. To help sooth and relax the ferret, gently swing him with the hand under his arms, and gently stroke his body by pulling it through the other hand. This method works with even the most un-cooperative of ferrets, even adults. With tamer ones, a few minutes of this treatment will induce a soporific state, rather like the 'dizzying' of a chicken or pigeon.

At first, ferrets that are not used to being handled may struggle and try to escape; at such times, do not increase the pressure on the ferret's body to try to prevent it from moving, as this may well cause injury to the ferret.

While holding it in your arms, give the animal a tit-bit, such as a small piece of meat. This is a very good way to win the ferret's confidence and get it to accept you — the beginnings of a good relationship and a good rapport.

Chapter 3

Housing

One of the most important aspects of keeping ferrets, and which must be given extensive consideration and action prior to the purchase of animals, is that of housing:

In the middle ages, it was common for ferrets to be housed in small wooden barrels; even today, some (too many!) owners keep their ferrets in cages which are either too small or of the wrong design — or both. There are two main types of ferret keepers — those who see their animals as pets, and those who see them as working animals. I accept that there are some who see their ferrets in both of these categories, but I hope that my readers will allow me this generalisation. Pet keepers tend to keep their animals indoors, while the keepers of workers tend to keep their charges outside the home. To avoid further confusion and perceived slurs, I will refer to the two categories as 'indoor ferrets' and 'outdoor ferrets'.

Indoor Ferrets

For ferrets kept inside the home, there is little need to make elaborate and totally weather-proof cages. Indeed, some owners simply leave their ferrets free to wander around the human home, with perhaps a pet bed or nest-box in a corner, and a cat litter tray where the animals can relieve themselves.

To many indoor ferret keepers, however, this is not sufficient; there are, after all, inherent dangers in allowing ferrets the run of the house. Human feet, especially when encased in heavy shoes or boots, do nothing for the well-being of ferrets, while the animals themselves may climb into danger areas or even bite electric cables.

If your ferrets are to be allowed total free access to all parts of the human home, you must take precautions to prevent their injury. These precautions include informing all visitors that ferrets are loose in the home, and ensuring that all cupboards, drawers etc are kept closed. It is also advisable to keep all outside doors and windows closed too; they can act has avenues of escape for the ferrets, but may also allow access to cats or other potential predators of your ferrets.

Minimum housing for this type of ferret keeping is a cat or dog bed and a litter tray (preferably in each room but, as an absolute minimum, one on each level of the human home). Better still is to provide a secure cage into which the ferret may be fastened as and when required.

This cage need not be elaborate or even heavy duty, since it will only act as a temporary holding cage, for example when you have guests, or in hot weather and when all windows and doors are left open. Nevertheless, the cage should be secure, and have an adequate supply of bedding available to the ferrets at all times.

Outdoor Ferrets

Obviously, ferrets living out-of-doors must be supplied with a fully weather-proof cage, which is big enough, and of the correct dimensions, to allow the ferrets to indulge in their natural behaviour. It may come as a surprise to some readers, but ferrets are three-dimensional animals; that is they like to climb.

One of the comments made when people first see my ferrets in their own cages, is that they have never before seen a ferret that climbs. Without exception, this is due to a lack of opportunity for the ferret, and not because my animals are unusual in their habits.

There are two main types of housing for ferrets; one is the 'ferret cub' (a hutch), and the other the 'ferret court' (an aviary type cage). Both have their adherents, and both have their place. My own ferrets all live in ferret courts throughout the winter, but in the summer, the hobs are all housed in separate cubs.

Whichever method of housing you choose to supply for your ferrets, you must remember that it will be home — in some cases a complete world — to the ferrets which are kept in that cage. It is obvious, therefore, that the cage should be a suitable size and shape, be easy to maintain and repair, and supply all of the items necessary for the ferrets to lead a long and happy life.

Ferret Cubs

In essence, these cages are simply well-built hutches, similar to the type that many rabbits are kept in. The minimum size for a cub suitable for two ferrets is 1.5m x 0.75m x 0.75m; it is better to err on the large size than give animals cramped quarters. A nest-box must also be supplied, and this can be fixed to the outside of the cub, thus giving more space for the ferrets to live, or may form an integral part of the cub. Access to the nest-box should be through a small 'pop-hole', measuring about five centimetres in diameter for jills, and seven to ten centimetres diameter for hobs.

A typical ferret cub, suitable for housing a ferret out of doors. (Shown without solid front door to nest-box, at left, and wire door to run)

41

Materials for the cub must be chosen with care, as they must;

— be easy to work with
— have good insulating properties
— be affordable
— be easy to maintain
— be non-porous, or at least capable of being made so
— be strong and durable, giving the cage a long life.

Without a doubt, the only material which comes close to fulfilling all of these criteria is wood. In this case, the cub should be built from exterior or marine quality plywood, at least one centimetre thick and screwed rather than nailed together, to enhance the strength of the structure. Do not paint the timber as this will make the cage 'sweat', and it will never really look clean. Instead, use one of the many brands of timber treatment sold for use on garden fences and outbuildings. Ensure that the material is one hundred per cent non-toxic, and follow the manufacturer's instructions implicitly. Re-treat on a regular basis. *Never* use creosote, as this is poisonous.

The roof should be sloping to the front, where it should overhang by about five centimetres; the slope will prevent the build-up of water on the roof, while the overhang will help prevent water from dripping into the cub via the wire front. The roof should be covered with top quality bitumen felt, or a similar material, to give complete water protection. To ensure ease of maintenance, cleaning etc, the top should be hinged, allowing it to be fully opened for cleaning, giving unrestricted access to the cub's interior. For safety's sake, fit a device which will be able to lock the lid open; more than one ferret has met an untimely death due to a gust of wind blowing down the lid of the cub.

A nice effective refinement is to make the roof double skinned, which helps insulate the cage interior from fluctuating ambient temperatures; this is particularly important in hot weather, as ferrets cannot tolerate excessive heat. Make the gap between the skins at least 150 mm, and this will act in the same way that double glazing works with windows.

If you have not given the roof a double skin, then there are temporary measures that you can take to cool the cub in hot weather. Place four thick pieces of timber, at least two centimetres thick, along each edge of the roof, and place a piece of sheet timber, exactly the same size as the roof, over these. Another method is to cover the roof with cloth or hessian sacking, and by keeping this material wet, the inside of the cub will remain at tolerable temperature levels. However, a little planning at the design stage of cub making will eliminate the necessity for such actions every summer.

All joints in the cub must be tight and well-fitting, with any gaps filled to prevent draughts. The front, which should also be hinged, should be covered with top quality weld mesh, at least 16 swg and with a mesh size of either 25mm x 25mm or 25mm x 10mm. If the mesh is any larger, kits will either be able to escape, or will get stuck while trying to; any smaller, and the mesh will not allow enough light and fresh air through.

A two-tier ferret cub, which helps utilise available space to the maximum.

To help ensure security, fit heavy duty hasps and staples, and use the very best pad-locks; there is always someone who will covet your possessions, and it is only common sense to take precautions to help prevent the theft of your ferrets.

Raise the cub off the floor by adding legs; this will help reduce temperature loss by cold striking up from the cold, damp ground, and also put the cub at a convenient height for you to work on, when cleaning and performing other maintenance duties.

Rather than waste the space below the cub, it is possible to turn it into an exercise area for the ferrets. This is easily achieved by covering the back and both sides with weld mesh, and putting a pair of opening doors on the front; the addition of a solid timber floor will complete the exercise area. The ferrets can gain access to this exercise area via a length of corrugated piping, such as that sold for draining soil. By providing a shutter which can seal off the access, along with a separate nest-box that can be placed in the bottom area, you will also have made a separate cub, for emergency use, or to separate ferrets in the breeding season.

I must here mention that some ferret keepers make all of the cub floor from wire mesh; I have never held with this practice, and feel that it serves no useful purpose for the ferret's welfare. The only possible benefit is to the idle keeper, who will not have to concern himself with cleaning the cub as often as he should; the wire floor will allow cold and draughts in to the cub, thereby making the occupants suffer. If owners cannot be bothered to keep the floors of their ferrets' cubs reasonably clean and dry, then I would question whether they should be keeping ferrets at all.

To ensure that one corner of the cub does not sink in to the ground, causing the cub to topple over, and that all debris from the cub is easily cleaned up, the area that the cubs stand on should be of either concrete or well laid paving slabs.

A suitable ferret cub, with the nesting-area above the run.

Another design of cub which is also suitable, but would benefit from being placed in an area where it would be sheltered from prevailing winds.

It is also worth investing in a proper path to the cub area, again made of either concrete or paving slabs; the benefits of this will be realised during bad weather, when rain and snow will turn any other type of well-used path into a sea of mud.

Ferret Courts

If you have the space, then ferret courts are much better — for both the ferrets and yourself — than cubs, and are to be commended.

The first ferret courts were built from brick or stone, and resembled dog kennels with runs attached. I have seen a few modern courts built on the same lines, although it is true to say that these are the exception rather than the rule. Most modern ferret keepers use timber, metal and plastics in the construction of both cubs and courts.

My own courts consist of a timber frame (50mm x 50mm), covered with 5 swg welded mesh. They vary in size from 4m x 4m to 2m x 1m, but all are 2m high. This height is as much convenience for myself, as it is a design consideration for the ferrets; at this height, I can easily stand and work in the court, without having to adopt a very uncomfortable crouching position. This ability ensures that cleaning and maintenance are easily achieved. However, as stated earlier, ferrets, although not as agile as their cousins the martens, do like to climb; the extra height means that the court can be furnished with branches for them to enjoy this activity, thus increasing their living space.

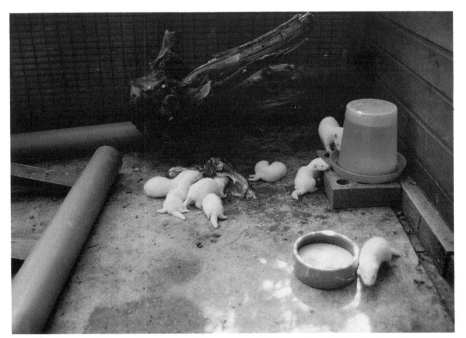

A business of ferrets in a court. The author believes that this is the best type of housing for all ferrets kept out-of-doors.

All of my courts have concrete floors. Some would argue that it would be more natural for the animals to be given a soil floor, complete with grass; such a floor may look nice when newly laid, but will soon become worn. In addition, ferrets also like to dig, and soil is an easy medium to dig in; escapes would be inevitable unless the welded mesh were sunk into the floor by at least 50cm. Another problem that grass and soil floors would have is one of cleanliness; it is impossible to keep such a surface clean and, when a disease occurs within the cage population, thorough disinfection of the surface is imperative to prevent the spread of the problem, but such cleaning is impossible to achieve on soil.

Concrete, on the other hand, is porous, and urine and other fluids can and do soak into the floor. It is possible to treat the concrete with paints and epoxy resins which are designed to seal the surface, making cleaning much easier. However, there have been several reports of animals kept on surfaces treated with some of these materials, which have succumbed to poisoning of various kinds. While I am sure that there are sealers which are perfectly safe for use with animals, I have yet to find one, and prefer instead to put up with the slight inconvenience of having a porous floor on my ferret courts.

In some of my ferret courts, nest-boxes are fitted inside, while on one, I have fitted all of the nest-boxes on the outside. This serves two purposes; it give the ferrets more room in their court, and allows me to inspect and clean the nest-boxes without the necessity to empty the cage of its occupants. I can easily lock the ferrets in their nests while cleaning the run, and out of them while cleaning the nest-boxes. I can also gain access to young, by placing the food for the mothers in the run, and then going out of the court to the nest-boxes and inspecting the kits; this helps alleviate stress on nursing mothers and kits alike.

Separate nest-boxes such as this one are essential in courts.

There should be enough nest-boxes for all the occupants to gain benefit from them; I always have one more nest-box than I do ferrets within the cage. This enables each one to gain access, even if one or more of the other ferrets decides to start bullying. The nest-boxes should measure about 45cm x 45cm x 30cm high, and be positioned around the court, preferably at different levels, but all with the pop-holes facing away from prevailing winds. If they are raised about 150mm off the ground, this will help protect them against draughts and cold. Securely fix a piece of timber about 40mm long to the nest-box entrance, and this will ensure that the ferrets can gain easy access. These ramps should be set at about thirty degrees, and have small wooden cross-pieces, or deep saw cuts, about every 25mm along their length. This will give the animals' feet extra purchase, and enable the ferrets to safely use the ramps even when the wood is wet and slippery.

I like to have a roof which opens on these nest-boxes, in order that I can check on any litters, and so build them in the manner of 'shoe boxes'. This gives easy access, and also helps prevent ingress of water, even in torrential rain. Place a good covering of wood shavings in the bottom of each nest-box to help absorb any water carried in on the animals' feet or fur; *never* use sawdust, as this can adversely affect the ferrets, causing breathing or eye problems. Ensure that each nest-box has an ample supply of top quality meadow hay, with more hay needed in very cold weather, and far less in warm weather. During extremely warm weather, the ferrets may well throw out most or even all of the hay, in order to keep their sleeping quarters at the correct temperature. I am of the opinion that it is better to supply too much than not enough bedding, leaving the ferrets to make their own beds according to the prevailing weather conditions.

Although ferrets enjoy fresh air, and both a little sunshine and rain, it is essential that they also have access to shelter from these two elements, without having to seek refuge in their nest-boxes. To give the ferrets shelter, I cover about a third of the roof of the court with corrugated polycarbonate sheeting; this is translucent, allowing light through, but not creating a 'greenhouse effect' in the court. Being impervious to moisture, it also keeps rain and snow out of the court. It is essential that all sheets used have a good overlap, to prevent water seeping through the joints, and that the whole roof slopes off to an adequate gutter and down pipe, allowing water to run away safely.

The inside of the court can be supplied with various items, such as branches, plants or bushes in tubs or even a rockery. These items will enhance the appearance of the court to human eyes, and also provide play items for the ferrets. Always ensure that any plants placed inside a court are not poisonous to the ferrets. Piles of rocks and lengths of piping (of different diameters) will help the ferret to learn to enter such places without any fear; while this is essential for working ferrets, it is also good fun for pet ferrets!

Positioning

The correct positioning of your ferret cub or court is of paramount importance, and should obviously be considered before construction of the cage begins. After all, the cage's inmates cannot move from that area and are, therefore, quite literally at the mercy of the elements. Ideally, the chosen site should give protection from excesses of wind, rain, sun, heat and cold.

It is impossible to give readers precise rules on where a cub or court should be placed, as everyone's situation will be different. When making your choice, however, there are certain facts that should be very carefully considered.

Remember that in cold weather, some sunshine will be extremely useful to keep the ferrets warm, but in the summer, that same sunshine will be unwanted, and may even prove fatal to the ferrets in that cage. Bear in mind too, that the sun moves throughout the day, and take advantage of this fact. Early morning sun is much cooler than that of midday, and it is usually possible to position the cage so that the inmates benefit from an early morning sunning, allowing them to, quite literally, warm up for the day ahead. However, do not have the sun on the cage at midday, so that the animals cook in the heat.

Ascertain the direction of the prevailing winds (which will, of course, drive the rain) and ensure that there is an adequate and effective windbreak. A trellis, covered with a non-poisonous creeping plant, will make an attractive and efficient windbreak and sun shield, and will be appreciated by the lady of the house and neighbours.

Cleaning

If you are to successfully keep ferrets for a long time, it is important that you instigate a sound cleaning regime, using the correct materials and tools. As mentioned earlier, this is far easier to achieve if you plan the design properly, and give great thought to the materials used in the construction of the cage, be it a cub or a court.

Although their critics would never admit or accept the fact, ferrets are extremely clean animals; they spend much time on personal hygiene and are very particular where they empty their bladders and bowels. The latrine area chosen by ferrets is almost always in a corner, or at least against a vertical edge, and as far away from their sleeping quarters as possible. Once established, the latrine will stay in the same location for the same ferrets. Where ferrets are kept in a commune or a business, ie three or more ferrets, there may well be more than one latrine, but the same ferrets will always use the same latrine.

This habit makes life easy for the ferret keeper, since part of his daily routine should be to shovel and scrape out the area of the latrine(s), thus reducing the build up of faeces, and thus smell and the risk of disease. In cubs, some owners cut a hole in the corner furthest from the nest-box, and cover it with weld mesh, of about 16swg and 10mm x 10mm. The theory is simple; the ferrets will use the area as a latrine, and the faeces will fall through the mesh into a suitable container placed under the mesh by the ferrets' owner. I have tried this, but have never witnessed much success; the faeces tend to get stuck on the wire, which is the very devil to clean! Much better, to my mind, to reinforce the area of the latrine with extra timber, plastic, stainless steel or even a few extra coats of timber treatment to protect it against the urine and faeces, and clean the area every day.

With a court the problems are much less, providing that you have given the floor the necessary slope to allow good drainage. Clean the latrine area every day and, once a week, remove all of the ferrets from the run, and use a power jet hose pipe to clean the whole area. After being left for about twenty to thirty minutes, the run will be dry enough to allow the ferrets back in.

A good quality disinfectant should be used to help reduce the build up of smells and harmful bacteria, but great care is needed in the choice of disinfectant. Disinfectant agents are classed as either physical or chemical, for example steam can be used to clean cages (common in kennels and catteries), and is a physical agent, whereas chemical agents are found in the disinfectants which we can buy from many shopping outlets. All disinfectants are potentially dangerous, and yet their labelling would often lead one to believe otherwise! Some are highly toxic to certain species, while all can have allergic reactions on certain individuals. All disinfectants work better at higher temperatures, and so should be mixed with hot water to form a solution of the correct ratio. *Never* mix two disinfectants together, as the results could be highly dangerous.

The chemicals used in disinfectants are classified into generic groups — alcohols, aldehydes, alkalis, halogens, phenolics and surface-active agents — and common disinfectants draw their constituents from the aldehydes (eg formalin), the halogens (eg sodium hypochlorite — bleach), and the phenolics (eg phenol). In addition, the surface-active agents are sub-divided into two more groups — quaternary ammonium compounds ('quats'), and amphoteric/polymer surface-active agents. The latter group is the one which contains the most recent additions of the disinfectants, and are both detergents and disinfectants, making them excellent for both cleaning surfaces and then rendering them 'safe'. I cannot recommend the use of these preparations enough in ferret cubs and courts.

There are two generic types of disinfectant generally available — sodium hypochlorite (bleach) and phenol.

Bleach

This is extremely effective and forms the basis of many 'cleaners' and 'disinfectants', all of which are cheap, easily available and, providing that common sense precautions are taken, relatively safe and, therefore, useful for cleaning ferret cubs and courts. Sodium hypochlorite has a very low residual toxicity; throughout the world it is used for cleaning dairy utensils and milking machines etc. It can, therefore, obviously be used for cleaning the ferrets' dishes and drinking bottles, provided that these are well rinsed before use.

It should be noted that all disinfectants are only effective when used on cleaned and rinsed surfaces, as even small amounts of detergent or organic material can inactivate sodium hypochlorite. Solutions of bleach and water, if left standing for any time, will also lose there efficacy, as the bleach oxidises and much is lost to the atmosphere. Because of this, it is important that all bleach solutions are used immediately they are prepared; if they are left standing, they will be totally ineffective against micro-organisms, and you may as well save your money and simply use a bucket of water!

After use of bleaches in ferret cubs and courts, rinse well with clean water, and then allow the cage to stand empty for about thirty minutes before returning the ferrets to their home.

Phenol

Popularly known as carbolic acid, phenol is a caustic poison which is extremely toxic to living tissue. Modern derivatives (all of which share the same properties as phenol) include xylenol, chloroxyphenol, orthophenylphenol and hexachlorophene and are equally dangerous to living tissue, being absorbed through the skin; an indication of the inherent danger of their use is that many of these substances have been banned from use in all products designed for human babies, and have long been *verboten* in catteries. When used in ferret cubs and courts, the animals may well suffer from sore feet, tales and tummies, and even 'burns' to their lips, mouths and tongues; ferrets will also die from phenol poisoning.

It is easy to tell if a disinfectant contains phenol, as it will turn white when added to water. If you care for your ferrets, DO NOT USE ANY PHENOL-BASED DISIN-FECTANT IN THEIR CAGE! To ignore this warning may well result in injury or death for all the ferrets in your keeping.

In the UK and most other countries, the labels on most disinfectant bottles and containers will list the chemical ingredients. However, in some countries, this is not so, and it is possible to see manufacturer's claims that the substance is 'safe', 'safe in use', or 'safe when used as directed'. I have never seen any label which claims that the disinfectant is safe for use with all animals and, even if this were to be true, there could still be individual animals which have an allergy to one or more of the chemical ingredients in the product.

Many disinfectants have added 'smell', usually pine or similar; while this may make the liquid more appealing to humans, it will only mask smells. Of course, if the cub or court is properly and regularly cleaned, there will be no need for this masking. In addition, heat may well cause irritant fumes to be drawn from untreated timber into which the disinfectant has soaked.

Whichever disinfectant you use, ensure that you adhere strictly to the manufacturer's recommended dilutions and, if any animal shows signs of an allergic reaction — change the disinfectant immediately!

Cleaning Utensils

Obviously, in order to carry out the day-to-day cleaning of one's ferret cub or court — essential to avoid health problems — certain items of equipment are needed. These need not be elaborate, and most homes will already have most items 'in stock'; however, it is advisable to have a totally separate set of cleaning utensils, which are to be used exclusively for the ferret cubs and courts. In order to minimise the spread of diseases between cages, it is highly recommended that a separate set is used for each cage, and that interchange of utensils does not occur. General items that you will require are listed below;

> Hard-bristled, long-handled broom
> Hard-bristled handbrush
> Dust pan/shovel
> Scraper (for cleaning latrine; a paint scraper is ideal)
> Buckets (stainless steel are best, although plastic will suffice)
> High-power hosepipe (or, even better, a pressure washer — see later)

Scrubbing brushes (deck scrubbing brushes with long handles are ideal for courts)

Pressure washers are designed to operate at either high or low pressures, using hot or cold water, or steam. They can be used with detergent, and are ideal for cleaning courts — roof, walls and floors.

Try to establish a routine, which will help you, and also ensure that the ferrets have well cleaned cages, thus helping them lead longer and healthier — and dare I say happier — lives. To reduce the risk of smells, keep two buckets by the door of the cage, one containing a mild solution of surface action cleaner, and the other fresh water; both buckets will require cleaning out and replenishing every few days. As the dirty feeding bowls are removed from the cub or court, wash and rinse them in the buckets.

Flies are always a nuisance in warm weather, and they are best tackled by keeping a strict cleaning regime, regularly clearing the latrines. In addition, suspending fly papers around the outside of the cub, or inside a court (providing that they are well out of the reach of the inmates), will help reduce the problem. Ferrets being natural hoarders will hide away bits of uneaten food, often, but not always, in their nest-box. In warm weather, maggots will appear within a few hours unless the cage is kept scrupulously clean and all of the surplus food removed regularly. Even where flies are a great nuisance, one should *never* use insecticidal sprays in or around an occupied cage.

Food Dishes and Water Bottles

Water is essential for all animals, and you should always make provision on the outside of the cub or court to attach a water bottle. This should be of the gravity feed type, complete with a stainless steel tube and nipple, and is far preferable to the traditional dish. Dishes can easily be tipped up — even quite heavy ones — and the water may soon become fouled and undrinkable, even if the dish is emptied, cleaned and replenished daily. It is also possible for young kits to fall into bowls of water and either drown or become seriously chilled. The tube to the bottle must be checked daily, in case it has become blocked. To help inhibit the growth of algae on the inside of the bottle (which is both unsightly and a health risk), a coloured bottle, such as a wine bottle, can be used.

Clean, fresh drinking water should always be available to ferrets, and is best provided via a drinking bottle with a stainless-steel spout.

Chapter 4

Handling, Taming and Training

Whenever I make one of my frequent public appearances with ferrets, I always manage to amaze my audience by handling the ferrets easily — and not getting bitten! Many of the onlookers will make remarks to the effect that I must be mad, or my ferrets have had all of their teeth removed. While I cannot comment on the first accusation, I can assure my readers that none of my ferrets have had teeth removed to facilitate handling

There is no secret behind my tame (or 'quiet') ferrets, other than the fact that they are constantly handled in the correct manner, and so neither party has anything to fear from the other. To me, this is purely common sense; I see no purpose in having an animal that one is fearful of handling, since this will mean that the animal is not handled at all, and neither will the cage be cleaned as often as it should be. All this will do is create an imprisoned animal, which will be aggressive through fear; it is cruelty to the ferret.

For some reason, there are those who deliberately create untamed and unhandleable ferrets. Their 'reasons' are either that they are to be used for hunting, or that it somehow makes the owner appear much more macho, having dominance over such a fierce animal. Neither of these are valid reasons. Ferrets used for hunting need to be just as manageable as pet ferrets; if you cannot handle a ferret in normal conditions, how will you fare when the ferret has had a fight with a rabbit or a rat, or is simply excited at the action? As for the second 'reason', I cannot justify even trying to explain the mentality of such people; all I will say is that such people should not be allowed to own any animal.

There is an old saying — 'You cannot teach an old dog new tricks'. This is not true — you can, providing that you are extremely patient and, of course, it will take more time. The same applies to ferrets. Over the years, I have had many ferrets brought to me, having been found wandering in the fields, or on roads, or even in the car parks of country fairs. Obviously, when the animals are first captured and brought to me, many of them are not handleable, as they are frightened and, in some cases, injured. However, in almost all cases, I have managed to tame the ferrets and I can honestly say that I have never been badly bitten by any ferret in my care.

I have, however, been bitten by other people's ferrets; this usually happens immediately after the owner has assured me that their ferrets are 'completely safe and totally trustworthy'. In almost every case where I have been injured, the ferrets in question exhibit clear evidence of mistreatment; some are half-starved, others have been injured in some way, while others have had some teeth removed, or even broken off. This latter practice is one which I abhor, and is still fairly

The author's son, Thomas (aged 2¾) with a couple of ferret kits. There is no danger to the child or kits when both are brought up together and treated with respect.

A muzzled ferret. It is not necessary to use such items — even if you do manage to fit one! The only ferret that the author has managed to fit one to is this one — and it's stuffed!

53

common throughout the world. Even where people have the ferret's teeth removed by a suitably qualified veterinary surgeon, and under anaesthetic, I still am not happy with such an action. Where people do it themselves, often using pliers, I become very angry, and wish that the perpetrators could endure such pain themselves.

One of the old ferret books that I own dates form 1897 (*Ferrets* by Nicholas Everitt), and this shows a form of 'coping' (muzzling) which involves stitching the ferret's lips together; he states that there is no cruelty involved! It may surprise the reader to know that today, almost one hundred years later, some people are still employing this method, although very few will ever openly admit to it. Even many of those who would — rightly — decry such practices as teeth breaking or extraction, or sewing a ferret's lips together as cruelty, will still employ muzzles or copes to prevent the ferrets from biting.

Why do people go to such lengths to prevent bites when the answer is so simple — do not give the ferret reason to bite! By regular, considerate handling, even the most 'aggressive' ferret will soon calm down.

I am a great believer that there is no such thing as a bad ferret, simply too many bad owners of ferrets!

Initial Handling

It is best for all concerned that handling should begin as early as possible; if you have bred a litter from your jill, the kits should be handled regularly from the time that their eyes are open and they are wandering around their cage. If the jill has been handled properly, and is truly tame, she will not usually object to this (see chapter 6).

Begin by gently stroking the kits, at the same time talking in low, soothing tones. After only a very short time they will accept, and even welcome, this attention. After a couple of days of this, pick up the kits (one at a time) by placing one hand around its chest, and the other under its back end. This will help ensure that the animal's weight is evenly distributed, and no undue pressures are exerted on the quite fragile body.

Having established an acceptance of your handling the kits, the next step is to get them to accept that your fingers are wonderful — but definitely not on the menu! To do this, mix a couple of raw eggs with some full cream milk; assuming that you are right handed, dip the fingers of your left hand into the mix, and offer them to the kits. The young ferrets will be attracted by the smell and will start licking your fingers. Some will become very excited, and may nip your flesh; at this age, the sensation is only mildly uncomfortable. However, you must not allow them to get away with this action, as they will think it is acceptable behaviour. Instead, as a kit nibbles your finger, gently flick him on the side of his face; this should be more of a shock to the kit, than actual pain. He will probably hesitate, and then recommence his nibbling; flick him again. After a few days of this treatment, none of the kits will even dream of biting your fingers. Hence, when the animals are strong enough to hurt you, they will have no desire to.

With adult ferrets the procedure is very similar, in that we are going to train him that certain actions are unacceptable. With rescued ferrets, which are very frightened, picking up may be quite difficult. The best way to achieve this is either with a gloved hand (a method that I never use), or by first pulling the animal firmly but slowly backwards, by the tail. This will make the ferret automatically dig in his front feet, and try to put his weight to the front. As he does this, take hold of his torso (keeping hold of his tail) with the other hand, placing the thumb and little fingers around the ferret's chest, under his arms. Keep the other three fingers behind his head. This is the best way I have ever found of securely and safely holding a struggling adult ferret.

To calm a ferret — of any age — hold him around his torso and gently swing him backwards and forwards, gently pulling his body through the half closed fist of the other hand. This stroking is something that all ferrets seem to enjoy, and it always calms them.

To teach an adult ferret not to bite takes a little more time and patience than it does for a kit. Holding him as previously described, offer the knuckles of your other hand; it is important that it is the knuckles and no other part of the hand, as there should be no loose flesh for him to grab hold of (bite). As he tries to bite you, quickly move your hand away, and gently slap or flick him on the side of the face; as with the kits, your intention should be to shock him rather than inflict physical pain.

Immediately after the slap, swing him again, as previously described. After a few minutes of swinging, offer him your knuckles again. As he tries to bite, slap him again. Repeat this process for about ten to fifteen minutes every day and, after two or three days, you should have a tame and handleable ferret.

Practice makes perfect, and I am of the opinion that no ferret can be too tame. I also have an allergy — to pain, which I find hurts!

Walking on a Lead

Many people take their ferrets for a walk and, as with dogs, they attach a lead to the animal for safety's sake. Obviously, the ferret does not take to the lead instantly, and it is worth spending a few moments to get the ferret accustomed to the collar and lead before starting the actual walk.

The collar for the ferret should be soft but strong, is usually made from either leather or nylon, and must be a secure fit. Every collar I have bought for my ferrets has required new holes for secure fastening, and I find a special leather hole punch to be an indispensable aid for this operation. While securely holding the ferret, place the collar around his neck and mark the place where the hole needs to be. Once you have punched the hole, you can try the collar on the ferret. Ensure that it is tight enough not to come over the animal's head, while not being so tight that the ferret cannot breathe. Once fitted, place the ferret on the floor; he will immediately try his hardest to get the collar off and so he should be distracted for five to ten minutes, by which time he will have forgotten the collar, and will thus accept it.

When this has happened, and not before, it is time to attach the lead to the collar. Again, the ferret will react to the new encumbrance, and so requires distracting until such time as it is accepted. Once this is achieved, you are ready to embark on your first walk together.

A pet ferret being taken for a walk on a lead. Note the harness, much better than a collar, and far more secure.

Don't be too ambitious; a thirty mile route-march will not be a happy occurrence for the ferret! The first few walks should be taken at a very leisurely pace, and not cover more than a few hundred metres. The ferret will keep stopping at every new smell and sight, and you may well have to drag him from some of them. Try to make the whole experience of the walk a pleasurable one, for both of you. Be patient and remember that the things which you take for granted, and to which you react in a blasé manner, will be entirely new and mysterious — maybe even frightening — to your ferret.

Training the Ferret to Come To You On Command

Another behaviour that amazes spectators at the events that I attend with my ferrets, is when the ferrets come to me on my command. For some reason, behaviour that is considered perfectly normal and commonplace in dogs, is looked on with awe when it occurs with ferrets.

All animal training is linked to conditioned reflexes; the reaction that the animal is conditioned to exhibit when it receives a certain stimulus. The great Russian physiologist, Ivan Pavlov, investigated conditioned reflexes in his famous experiments of the late nineteenth and early twentieth centuries. He noticed that he could induce the production of saliva in dogs by the sight, smell and taste of food; he then linked the appearance of food with an external stimulus — a bell ringing. After a while, he found that saliva production could be induced simply by ringing the bell.

When you go to feed your ferrets, habitually make the same noise(s). I always rattle my keys, while at the same time making a kissing noise, by pursing my lips together and sucking in through them. I do this as I come down the garden path to the courts, and continue it until I am actually giving the food to the ferrets, who obviously come to associate the noises with food; ie they are conditioned. After a few days of doing this, the ferrets will come out of their nest-boxes, and to the door of the court, on hearing one or more of the noises. Even when playing on the lawn, the ferrets will still run to me when they hear these noises.

Chapter 5

Feeding

To many people, the feeding of their ferrets is a matter that is given very little thought; as long as 'food' can be obtained at the right price, the matter is never discussed. However, the correct diet — balanced to give the right amounts of the relevant constituents — is essential for a long and healthy life.

Not so many years ago most ferret owners fed their animals on milk sops (bread and milk); some misguided or uncaring people still do so today! Speaking to these people, one hears several different 'reasons'. The first is that, if one fed meat to a ferret, it would give the animal a taste for flesh — and the animal would be more than inclined to bite the hand of anyone who came near, making the ferret totally untameable, or the ferret would make an extra effort to catch the rabbits it was chasing in the burrow. The second 'reason' given is that milk sops are the natural diet for ferrets. Neither argument, of course, is true.

I am amazed at how many people really do believe these theories, and how many can conjure up 'reasons' to justify the diets given to their animals. How on earth anyone can think that milk sops are natural for a ferret beggars belief; how often have you ever seen a ferret buying bottles of milk and bread in a shop — how else could they obtain such items?

Some owners give their animals a diet which they believe to be correct, without ever investigating the animal's nutritional requirements; as stated earlier, the main reason for most of these diets is their low cost!

I have spent a great deal of time and effort in researching all matters pertaining to ferrets, including their nutritional requirements. I have been amazed (and worried) by the results of some of this research. There is an old saying — 'You are what you eat' — and I believe that this also applies to ferrets.

Over the years I, like many others, have tried to find a good diet for my ferrets; good in that it is healthy for them, affordable for me, and readily available. I have probably tried most ferret diets except milk sops, which I have never believed in as I am only too aware of the nutritional deficiencies of such a diet. Fed a proper diet, the ferret's faeces will be very dark, solid and have little smell, and the ferret will probably live for ten or more years (I have had several ferrets which have lived to thirteen-plus years). When fed milk sops, the faeces are almost liquid, very pale in colour and extremely smelly; in human terms it is rather like living with perpetual diarrhoea — not a pleasant prospect! In addition, the ferret will lead a very unhealthy and short life (about three to five years).

Kits eating a complete food — biscuits which are designed to give the animal a complete diet, without the addition of anything else, other than water. Such feeds are not available in every country.

A Balanced Diet

Before going any further, it is worth considering what constitutes a 'balanced diet'. All animals require certain items in their diet, with quite large differences between species. All animals require water, fat/carbohydrate, protein, fibre, some minerals and some vitamins. A ferret fed on a truly balanced diet will lead a long, active and healthy life, more than repaying you for the cost of its diet. The main components of any diet are proteins, vitamins, minerals, carbohydrates, fats and fibre.

Protein

Proteins, or amino acids, are essential for growth and tissue maintenance, and should form at least thirty per cent of the ferrets' diet. They are present in meat, eggs and milk. There are many different proteins, all consisting of different arrangements of about twenty amino acids, but it is not necessary to differentiate between them here.

It should be obvious that while all ferrets require a high protein diet, it is even more important when considering nursing mothers, their kits and young ferrets in general. Likewise, males used for stud also require a higher protein content in their diet.

Carbohydrates

Carbohydrates provide the body with heat and material for growth. As they are made up of carbon, hydrogen and oxygen (which combine to form cellulose, starch and sugar), excess amounts are stored as fat in the body, often leading to obesity. As everyone knows, this can cause medical problems and difficulties in the ferrets' breeding; a fat, overweight ferret will not be as active, nor as agile as he should be, and so will not be as happy.

Vitamins

Vitamins are chemical compounds, essential for growth, health, normal metabolism and general physical well-being. Many vitamins play an important part in completing essential chemical reactions in the body, forming parts of enzymes — chemical catalysts. Some vitamins form parts of hormones, which are the chemical substances that promote the health of the body and reproduction.

There are two main types of vitamin — water-soluble and fat-soluble.

Water-soluble vitamins cannot be stored in the body, and so the day's food must contain the day's requirements of these vitamins. Fat-soluble vitamins can be stored in the body and, if too many are taken in at one time, they can be stored for use when the body needs them. However, an excess of such vitamins may cause toxic levels to accumulate in storage areas such as the liver. It is important to remember that an excess of any fat-soluble vitamin can lead to long term physical problems. You should also remember that a lack of essential vitamins can be detrimental to the ferret's health.

The ferret requires;

> *Water* — essential for all life
> *Protein* (30%) — for tissue and muscle growth and repair
> *Fat* (15 — 40 %) — for heating the body, and providing energy
> *Calcium* (1%) — for teeth and bones
> *Phosphorous* (1%) — for teeth and bones
> *Salt* (1%) — a vital mineral which acts as an electrolyte regulating the balance of water inside and outside cells
> *Fibre* (20—25%) — as an aid to digestion
> *Vitamin E* (about 250 mg/kg) — promotes normal growth and development, acts as an anti-blood clotting agent, and promotes normal red blood cell production.

Vitamin E is found in the yolk of eggs and in certain vegetable oils. A lack of this vitamin can cause infertility, heart and circulation problems and skin complaints.

Fat provides the ferret's body with energy but, given too much, the body will store it in the tissue. This can lead to many problems, including mating difficulties, heart problems and the re-absorbtion of foetuses.

Fibre (or roughage, as it used to be called) is essential for the well-being of the ferret's digestive system. Fibre will keep the ferret 'regular' and this will help prevent many of the diseases — including cancer of the bowel — with which some ferrets are afflicted. Fibre for the ferret is to be found in the fur and feathers.

The mineral calcium is found in liver, milk and milk products, egg-shells, fish and snails. It is also to be found in the bones and teeth of all animals. Phosphorous is found in liver, milk and milk products, and fish.

Diets

Ferrets are carnivores, a word derived from the Latin *carnis*, meaning flesh, and *vorare*, to devour. As such, their natural diet is one of flesh, ie whole carcasses of mammals, birds, reptiles, fish, amphibia and even some invertebrates. Without a doubt, the best diet for ferrets consists of complete cadavers of mammals and birds, although little harm is done by gutting these first, as long as the lungs, heart, liver and kidneys are left for the ferrets. Removing the guts and gut contents is useful, as it helps reduce the mess left in the cage, and the ferrets are highly unlikely to eat these items (they are, after all only thin skin filled with waste material), unless they are *very* hungry! All cadavers given, however, should be left in their skin/feathers, as this provides the ferret with essential fibre.

Do not, however, throw a complete cadaver into the ferrets' cage and leave it until it is all eaten. Such practices, which are all too common, are bad husbandry and will, eventually, lead to illness and possibly the death of one or more of your ferrets. Unless you keep a reasonable amount of ferrets in one court, rabbits should be cut into portions of various sizes, all with the fur left on. Leave the rabbit's organs inside, but check for such diseases as liver fluke (visible as white dots on the infected animal's liver), rejecting any such organs. If you have six or more ferrets in a court or a litter of kits which are eating flesh, a full rabbit, minus its guts, will be perfectly acceptable and will help the development of the kits.

Unless one has the opportunity and good fortune to have access to large areas of land — and the animals and birds that live there — this kind of diet can seem impossible to supply. Do not despair! There are acceptable alternatives.

Road casualties can a good source of food for ferrets; I have even seen feral ferrets and wild polecats eating such animals. On journeys through the countryside of most western countries, an alert driver will spot many dead animals by the roadside. These are usually rabbits, pigeons or similar species, with the occasional songbird and rodent. Wild rodents should not be fed to ferrets unless you can be reasonably sure that they are free from disease and have not been poisoned. Even then, the cadavers should be thoroughly gutted and inspected before feeding, but I would not recommend their feeding to ferrets, as the risks of infection and poisoning are so great.

Never feed 'old' meat from bodies that have been on the roadside for more than a few hours, as the flesh of these animals or birds may already be infected with the *clostridium botulinum* bacteria, the cause of botulism, a disease which is almost always fatal to ferrets. Always check the cadaver of any road casualty for signs of illness — puffy eyes, festering sores and/or poor fur, skin or feathers — and discard all that are suspect.

Many road casualties are young animals, who simply have not had the chance to learn of the dangers of the world and these of course, are ideal to feed to the ferrets.

Friends and farmers who shoot can often be relied upon to provide the cadavers of pest species, or even game species which are too badly shot for human consumption or have been badly chewed by a hard-mouthed dog. If you use your ferrets for hunting, then your own catch can also be utilised. There will, however, come times when this is still not enough to provide all of the food for your ferrets; a regular supply of good quality food is required for the animals' well-being, and your peace of mind.

Day-Old Cockerels

One of the items which I used to believe was good for ferrets was day-old cockerels (chicks). These are widely available, as they are the culled male birds from hatchings of eggs to supply new stock to egg producers. They are sold mainly as food for raptors — owls, hawks etc — and their cost is extremely low, as I can currently buy them for about £20 per thousand, or 2p each. A fully grown hob will eat two or three of these dead chicks each day, with a jill obviously eating less, making the total cost of a week's supply about 50p per ferret. However, there are great risks to ferrets fed on a diet in which day-olds feature greatly.

Research indicates that day-old chicks are very low in calcium, protein and fat, and contain very little vitamin E. The feeding of day-old chicks has also been shown to cause such problems as hypocalcaemia, actinomycosis (a thickening and swelling of the neck), osteodystrophy, thiamine deficiency, posterior paralysis (the 'staggers'), and other maladies (see chapter 9).

Prior to my research on the subject, I was feeding my ferrets with day-olds about every other day. After my research, I changed this, and now feed them no more than once or twice a week, and never feed day-olds to kits under ten weeks of age.

Dog and Cat Foods

A ready supply of quality meat is always available from supermarkets, in the shape of tinned dog and cat food, and many ferreters use this as a basis for their ferrets' diet. However, these are obviously not designed for ferrets, and many will need to have vitamin and mineral supplements added before they can be fed. Your veterinary surgeon will be able to offer you sound advice as well as provide the necessary supplements, if they are required.

Many pet shops now sell 'pet meat' or brawn, of different flavours, and some of these brands can be fed, but again, many will require supplementing to ensure no long term ill-effects if these items are to be given to your ferrets regularly or over a long period.

At the very least, I recommend that all tinned dog and cat foods (and other similar foods) be supplemented with the addition of bonemeal powder to ensure that the ferrets receive adequate amounts of calcium, vital to the well-being of the ferrets as it is essential for the animal to grow strong bones and teeth.

Dry Foods

The modern trend in animal nutrition is to feed 'complete diets', and in the zoos, where the idea started, and for dogs and cats, these are now the most popular types of feeding. The foods are usually made in pellet or 'muesli type' form. Initially, the idea was driven by necessity, as zoos needed to be able to supply a wide range of animals with all of their nutritional requirements, and found it almost impossible to do so by feeding 'natural' foods, many of which were just not available locally, or on a regular basis. The idea was highly successful and it was not long before the pet trade took an interest in the idea.

At first, the idea of feeding one's dog or cat with pellets or 'porridge' caused many people to avoid such foods but, eventually, the public discovered for themselves the merits of such diets. They are very convenient, have very little smell, are acceptable to all but the most pampered dog or cat and really are a 'complete diet'. Add to that cheapness, ease of availability and storage, and the fact that tinned pet foods contain a lot of water, and it is obvious why they have become so successful. However, unless you can obtain complete ferret diets, ie those designed specifically for the ferret, you will have to add supplements and be ever watchful for long-term deleterious effects on the ferrets. Such effects could be so insidious that they are difficult to notice until it is too late, by which time complete kennels of ferrets could have been made useless. In some countries, such as the United States, it is possible to buy a complete (dry) diet for ferrets, but this is not available in the UK at present.

A warning of embarking on untested diets was given by BP Nutrition (UK) Ltd, at a symposium organised by the Association of British Wild Animal Keepers (Management of Canids and Mustelids, 1980). In the paper presented to the meeting, the story was told of mink farmers using a commercial diet for their animals which had not been proven with mink. At first, everyone was happy with the results but, after more than eighteen months of being fed on this diet, the mink began to exhibit serious problems, including stunted growth, poor fur, and reduced litter sizes. We should learn the lesson and not feed items or diets which are not intended for our ferrets.

One of the advantages with feeding diets based on dried materials is that they tend to produce more solid, drier and less smelly faeces, and this encourages a lot of ferret owners to supply them to their charges. If you are tempted to try these diets with your ferrets, then do so carefully, and never feed dog or cat diets as a staple for long periods.

Chicken

Some years ago, I moved home to a small village in a new area, and found myself in the position of having over a dozen ferrets and no ferreting! Not only was I deprived of my favourite sport, I also had to find an alternative supply of food for the ferrets. As it was spring and my jills were pregnant, I had to find a good, reliable source quickly; young ferrets seem to have an unseemly appetite and this acted as a spur to my efforts.

I was shopping in the local village when I discovered a delicatessen which sold roasted whole chickens. Asking to speak to the shop's manager, I soon discovered that all of the chickens arrived at the shop complete with their giblets, which were then removed and discarded as waste material. I saw the opportunity and grabbed it with both hands, offering to collect all of these unwanted giblets on a regular basis; the manager also felt that this was his lucky day and he eagerly accepted my offer, telling me that I was doing him a great favour! I later discovered that the shop had received several complaints about smells caused by the decomposing giblets, especially during the warm weather. To ensure that no-one was ever left in the lurch, I always collected the giblets on a regular basis, even though on some occasions I did not need them; at such times they were simply burned in the garden incinerator.

My work has forced me to live in many parts of the UK and I frequently encounter problems acquiring a good, reliable source of food for my ferrets. In 1990 I moved to Derbyshire and once again had to think about food for my business of ferrets. As I live in the middle of farming country, I checked local business directories for farms which specialise in the production of eggs. It was not long before I found one who was willing — and even keen! — to help me. As the reader is probably aware, chickens only have a limited life for laying eggs at the frequency and quality demanded by today's farmers, who are businessmen. Once their useful life is over, they are disposed of. You may or may not agree with this course of action, but it is reality, and I believe in making the best of all situations. After arranging to meet him, we came to an agreement whereby, when he had a certain number of chickens which had reached the end of their working life, he would sell them to me for, quite literally, pennies.

Opportunities like these exist throughout the world and I can recommend that they are taken; however, it is important that, once you have made an agreement you abide by it, or you will find yourself having to find another source of ferret food.

Beware of feeding capons to your ferrets; these are birds which are chemically sterilised and, by feeding such birds (or parts of them) to your ferrets, you may cause all kinds of problems. There is some evidence that the hormones contained in these birds can cause congenital deformities in ferrets.

Poultry in general is easily infected with harmful bacteria and is often traced as the source of outbreaks of food poisoning; take care when feeding it to your ferrets. If chicken, or any other meat for that matter, has already been frozen but has now defrosted, never re-freeze it, as this will almost certainly cause health problems to the animals to which this re-frozen meat is fed. All frozen meats must be thoroughly defrosted before feeding, and then it must be fed immediately, to help to ensure that such ailments as botulism do not affect your stock. If you are not sure about any meat, boiling it for about fifteen minutes before feeding it to your ferrets will kill harmful bacteria.

Other Foods

Raw green tripe, the unprocessed stomachs of cows, is an excellent food for dogs, cats, ferrets and almost every other carnivore. In some countries, it is easily obtainable, with some pet shops selling it in 'tubes', minced, frozen and even in tins.

However, since the BSE ('mad cow') outbreaks in the UK, it has become very difficult to obtain large quantities of green tripe directly from abattoirs.

Tripe also has a very strong and disagreeable smell; many people will not feed it, solely for this reason. Ferrets, however, are not deterred by the smell, and will eat it with gusto. As with all meat, always ensure the tripe is fresh, and if frozen defrosted thoroughly, feeding it as soon afterwards as possible.

Heart, lights (lungs), cheek and udder can be bought reasonably cheaply and make good ferret food, but again its availability is being limited by the BSE scares. Liver is enjoyed by all ferrets and has much nutritional value; however, it should not be fed in excess and *never* form a staple. Avoid liver, often sold as 'pet food', which has been branded as 'unfit for human consumption', for whatever reason. My personal maxim is that if meat is not fit for me to eat, it is not fit for my ferrets either.

Many butchers, supermarkets, pet stores and other retailers sell 'minced pet food'. This usually consists of many different sorts of meat minced up together and frozen, and will often include offal, fat and waste. It is an open invitation for harmful bacteria; therefore it must be fed immediately it has been properly defrosted. If in any doubt as to its suitability, boil it for at least fifteen minutes before feeding it. These meats also tend to be high in fats and should not be fed as a staple, although the high fat content will be useful in cold weather or when the ferrets are working hard, as their calorific needs will be much higher than normal.

Fish is relished by ferrets but should only be fed in limited quantities; avoid smoked, salty or fatty fish. My own ferrets are given occasional small pieces of cod and whiting. All fish must be well filleted, as fish bones can easily become lodged in a ferret's windpipe, often with fatal results.

Eggs
In the wild polecats eat eggs, and so some ferrets keepers argue that these must, therefore, be good for ferrets as they are 'natural'. They then proceed to feed their ferrets with a regular diet of eggs, sometimes giving each ferret a full egg every day. What these people do not realise, is that in the wild, birds only lay their eggs at one time of the year — spring. It is only when birds are brought into captivity and their photoperiod manipulated, that they will supply eggs throughout the year.

Too many raw eggs (ie more than one per week for an adult ferret) will have a bad effect on ferrets; they can cause diarrhoea and even hair loss. Try feeding hard-boiled eggs, complete with their shells, which are a good source of calcium, or even scrambled eggs. Ferrets love them!

Adjusting the Diet

Don't forget that the animal's diet will have to be adjusted to compensate for its lifestyle; a ferret kept indoors and not given much exercise will need far less energy food (ie fat) than an animal kept outside and worked regularly. All animals will need more fat in colder weather. Pregnant jills and young kits will require higher amounts of protein and calcium.

Ferrets should be fed daily, and fasted one day each week; with my own stock, this is on Sundays. A fasting day is good for the health of all animals — including human beings.

How much food should a ferret be given each day? This is a very difficult question to answer, as it will vary from season to season, and from day to day, depending on ambient temperatures, energy expended by the ferrets, and many other factors. A general rule of thumb is to feed the ferrets with an amount which you think is correct, and then check on the food about an hour later. If all of the food has been eaten, always remembering that ferrets are hoarders, and some may have been secreted away in the nest-box or elsewhere, feed a little extra next time. Ideally, there should still be a small amount of food left about an hour after putting the food in the cage. Some people decry this as wasteful, but I prefer to ensure that all of my ferrets have sufficient food for their needs, rather than try to save a few pennies. All left-overs must be removed at the end of each day.

As the ferret's digestive system, like that of all carnivores, is quite short, too large a quantity of food will result in much of it passing undigested through the ferret. This is one reason why it is not satisfactory to feed the ferrets with one large meal every couple of days. Ferrets, like most animals, appreciate regular meals, and this will result in less waste; less opportunity for the food to go off before the ferrets have a chance to eat it; less illness amongst the ferrets, and happy and contented animals.

In the summer, when it is warm, I always feed my stock in the evening; this helps prevent the food from going off before the ferrets have a chance to eat it.

Water

Clean, fresh water is essential for all animal life, and so must always be available to your ferrets. Water is even more important to ferrets fed on a dry or semi-moist diet. It is best delivered in a drinking bottle with a stainless steel spout; many pet shops sell one-litre size 'rabbit drinking bottles', which are ideal. The bottles should be checked daily, ensuring that the water flows freely, as the spout can easily become blocked with wood shavings, hay and even fur. Ensure that the bottle is securely fastened to the cage, on the outside. Dark coloured glass, such as wine bottles, are a good method of slowing down the growth of algae on the inside of the bottle.

Regular checks must be made on all water bottles, especially in extremes of weather. During periods of very low temperatures the water in the bottles may well freeze, and often this will cause a glass or plastic bottle to crack. Covering the bottles with insulating material such as is designed for water pipes is a good way of preventing this; the one drawback with this is that it is impossible to check the contents of the bottle without physically removing the covering every time. This is, however, a small price to pay for the peace of mind of knowing that the water is unlikely to freeze.

In courts, where there are several ferrets living together, it is essential to have two or three bottles and maybe even a water container such as is given to chickens.

Always remember that variety is the spice of life; whatever diet you decide to feed your ferrets, vary it from time to time. This will keep the ferrets happy and healthy, and they will return the favour by working and playing even harder! A well thought-out, properly balanced diet will help keep your ferrets free from illness and disease. While this is obviously good for the ferret, it is also good for you, as it will mean less hassle and fewer vet's bills!

Chapter 6

Breeding

In some countries, almost all ferrets sold to members of the public have been neutered. Some suppliers claim that this is done to help the owners and prevent certain illnesses related to females which are not mated every year; some even claim that this practice reduces or eliminates smells and removes all aggressive instincts from the ferrets, particularly the hob. However, the main reason for the practice seems to me to be to prevent the ferrets being used for breeding.

For the rest of us, however, breeding is essential if we are to develop our idea of the perfect ferret, thus producing our own blood lines, as do breeders of dogs, cats and even racehorses.

Why Breed?

Before embarking on any project, it is always wise to ask yourself why you are doing it and what you wish to achieve; the breeding of any animals is a project which requires long and careful consideration, and must always be carried out for a valid reason. For most of us, that valid reason is the continuing quest for our elusive goal — the perfect ferret.

When I began with ferrets over a quarter of a century ago, I was lucky in acquiring a trio (one male and two females) which were of good breeding and looks. However, within a couple of years, I was sure that there was scope (and to my mind a need) for improvement. I was using the ferrets for rabbiting and had encountered a few problems which I associated with the size of the ferrets I was using; I considered them to be too large. My theory was — and still is — that if a ferret is too big, it cannot move quickly enough down the long and winding tunnels of a burrow. Worse still, if the rabbit runs into a 'stop' (a cul-de-sac), a large ferret can do nothing other than scratch away at the rabbit until the luckless bunny is dead, by which time the ferret is tired and hungry, and will eat her fill before curling up and going to sleep. Conversely, a ferret that is too small may well not have the physical resources to work for long enough periods to be of use, and may even be dragged around the burrow by a large rabbit that she manages to sink her teeth into.

I decided that I would produce my own 'line' of perfect rabbiting ferrets.

You may not wish to have such lofty and egotistic ideas, but simply want to have more ferrets like the ones which you now own, or you may wish to increase the number of ferrets and don't want to buy any. Do not, however, make the mistake of believing that you can make money out of ferret breeding; unless you have huge numbers, and operate a proper business, you will never make any money from such an undertaking.

Record Keeping

To my mind, one of the most vital items that you must have for any breeding programme is a good record-keeping system; by 'good', I mean accurate, up-to-date, efficient and effective. Such records are indispensable for fixing a new mutation or for selecting suitable breeding stock. By using the records carefully, it is possible to select stock that will produce good quality kits, or always produce large (or always small) litters. It is a sad but true fact that very few breeders of small animals keep any records at all, and the number who keep *good* records is almost non-existent.

There are various methods which you can utilise, from note-books to card indexes, loose-leaf pads to personal computers. I am well known as a 'gadget man', but I will only continue to use such items if they really are useful to me. The most valuable asset that any of us possesses is time; if by using a 'gadget' I can save myself some time, I feel that I should do so. With all new equipment and procedures, however, one must remember that there is always a learning curve — often quite steep — and so it will take time and effort before one is fully conversant with the equipment or procedure; only when you are fully conversant with it will you begin to reap any benefits.

It is imperative, if you are to be successful in your ferret breeding, that you maintain complete and accurate records from day one. These records can be kept on a card affixed to each cage, and/or in a book or some other central device. Whatever method you use, the record should contain the following information;

> Variety
> Name and/or reference number
> Breeder, if applicable
> Date of birth
> Parents, grandparents, and great-grandparents
> Siblings
> Breeding/mating details (including sizes of litters)

If you attach cards to the ferret cages, you will be able to see at a glance every relevant detail about the cage's inmates. All writing on these cards should be done using an indelible (waterproof) pen, since other inks will run when damp or when water is spilled on them. Never use pencil, as the writing will fade and you will have lost all of the information. Never trust to memory either, as it can fail all too often.

Not all of the above details need be written on the card on the ferret's cage, but all (and more) should be recorded in the 'stud-book', a central record (not necessarily a book) of all details pertaining to your ferrets. Without such a record, you will never to able to breed your animals successfully in an ordered and efficient manner. Neither will you be able to perpetuate a mutant colour, thereby risking losing it for ever.

It is a matter of convention that all males are given letters of the alphabet for recording purposes, while females are given numbers. This is due to the fact that, on average, more jills than hobs will be kept. Some breeders combine these codes to identify any litters produced from a mating. For instance, if ferret 'A' (male) is mated with ferret '1' (female), and this mating produces a litter of two males and one female, the males will be coded 'A1A' and 'A1B', and the female '1A1'. In the case of the male 'A1A', the A1 denotes that the parents are A and 1, and that the specific animal is a male, which is given a letter of the alphabet as its reference; the second male from the same litter will be A1B. I find this method too complicated and fussy to maintain. Instead, I simply number all my females from '1' to infinity, and the males 'A' to 'Z'; when I get to the end of the alphabet for the first time, I start again, prefixing all letters with the first letter of the alphabet, eg 'AA', 'AB', 'AC', 'AD', etc. When I get to the end of the alphabet for the second time, I prefix the letter with the second letter in the alphabet, eg 'BA', 'BB', 'BC', 'BD', etc. When I come to the end of the alphabet for the 26th time(!), I prefix the letter with two 'A's, eg 'AAA', 'AAB', 'AAC', 'AAD', etc.

The Stud-book

Many breeders use a loose-leaf folder for their stud-book, and are quite happy with this arrangement. However, when using such books, it is very easy for a page to be lost. A hard-backed note-book of A4 size is ideal, and you will have no trouble with pages going missing. Either enter the details of the females at one end of the book, and those of the males at the other end, or use two separate books. A typical page may be set out as follows

---

NAME: REFERENCE:

VARIETY:

DATE OF BIRTH:

BREEDER:

PARENTS:

PATERNAL G. PARENTS: MATERNAL G. PARENTS:

PATERNAL G.G. PARENTS: MATERNAL G.G. PARENTS:

SIBLINGS:

NOTES:

MATING AND BREEDING RECORD:

Computers

Many households now have a personal computer (PC), and this can easily be used to store records, indeed the main advantage with using PCs for record-keeping is the ease with which relevant information can be retrieved and displayed. These computers may be in the form of desk-top, lap-top, note-book or even pocket sized; the latter are often referred to as palm-tops or organisers. I find that a palm top, which can easily fit into a pocket, is extremely useful for recording details while one is actually with the ferrets. With suitable software, this information can be 'up loaded' onto the PC back in the warmth of the home. Of course the PC itself is useless without the appropriate software, and so the choice of this software must be given thought.

For record-keeping, some form of database is needed. This can, if the operator understands the system thoroughly, be very complicated and give many facilities which can prove invaluable. On the other hand, it is quite possible to buy software which is perfectly adequate, and which is user-friendly.

This type of software has a 'form-making' facility, enabling the operator to design his own blank standard form (eg pedigree, breeding record etc). The computer then stores both the blank and completed forms, enabling the operator to refer to records already written up (changing or adding to them if necessary), as well as displaying a blank form for completion if the operator wishes.

All records kept on computer have the advantage of being easily accessible, provided that some thought is given to their format, the fields chosen, and their storage. Even if your PC has a hard disk, it is still essential that you 'back-up' your information (and software) after every use of the PC. Ideally, you should have the original software, a copy loaded on to your hard disk and a 'back-up' copy. It is bad practice to store any data on the hard disk, as one fault can mean the loss of everything. Use floppy disks for all data storage, and have at least one 'back up' copy; the ideal is two such copies, one of which is stored in a separate building to the other, as insurance against fire or other such damage. There is also a risk that a hard disk will 'crash' and lose all of the information stored on it. While this is certainly not an everyday occurrence (thank goodness!), it does occasionally happen and, if you have not backed up your files, then you will be in a sorry state. As stated earlier, if you are storing data on your hard disk, such a crash may cause you to lose all of the information that you have gathered over many years, and so backing up should be a regular habit and carried out *every* time that you use your computer.

Remember also to keep all floppy disks away from sources of magnetism, since the information on them is stored by using magnetism, and external sources can corrupt the information, rendering it useless. Televisions, hi-fi speakers and video recorders are just some of the everyday items that are also powerful sources of magnetism.

Line-breeding and Inbreeding

Inbreeding is the mating together of closely related animals, eg mother to son, father to daughter, brother to sister. There is a commonly held belief that inbreeding is highly undesirable, resulting in poor stock and small litters. This is not true. *Controlled* inbreeding is the method that has been used for countless generations to produce champion racehorses, cattle and dogs. If inbreeding was deleterious *per se*, then we would have no Syrian ('golden') hamsters in captivity, as the original stock from which the vast majority of today's hamsters have descended came from one female found in Syria in 1930. The only dangers with inbreeding occur when there is little or no control, or when not enough animals are available to allow selective breeding. *Controlled* inbreeding will fix good characteristics, and bring out others which are not readily apparent.

Line-breeding is a less acute form of inbreeding, in which more distantly related animals are mated, eg cousins, grandparents to grandchildren etc.

New colour mutations are more likely to appear through inbreeding, as there is more likelihood that both animals in a mating will possess the same recessive mutant gene (see chapter 10 'Genetics', for more details).

In practice, most breeders use a combination of the two methods, keeping their own animals which are usually bred together (ie inbreeding), and occasionally borrowing a stud hob from another breeder — an 'outcross'. This is an animal that is entirely unrelated to its mate, and so will possess totally different genes; the introduction of unrelated blood is said to supply 'hybrid vigour'. According to some adherents of the theory, hybrid vigour will result in the offspring being tougher, more fertile, able to produce bigger and better litters, be less susceptible to illness and disease, and generally be fitter for survival. I feel that the idea has become overstated by many and is not the panacea that some would have us believe. The use of a 'shared' hob holds many dangers, particularly from the spread of disease.

The big danger with an outcross is that the animal could introduce genes which, although not showing any deleterious effect on that animal, when combined with the genes of other ferrets could prove disastrous. Again *control* is needed in all breeding programmes, if success is to be achieved.

Selection of Breeding Stock

There is an old stockman's saying about breeding animals that is as true for ferrets as it is for cows, horses, dogs or any other type of animal; 'Put the best to the best, and hope for the best!'

For your breeding to be successful, you must start your programme with the best animals that you can obtain. If you do not own animals of the best calibre, then you should seriously consider buying young stock, rather than breed your own animals from mediocre stock since, to coin another adage, 'you will only get out what you put in'. In other words, poor stock bred with other poor stock will only produce more poor stock.

A half-way house between breeding your own ferrets from your own stock and buying animals that another breeder has bred, is to borrow a top grade male (a stud) to mate with one of your females (the male in a mating is known as the 'sire', while the female is known as the 'dam'). Your female must, of course, be of a high standard, or you will simply be wasting your time. You will probably have to pay some price for the stud services of the male (although some breeders will give you this service for free, simply because they value the ferret fancy and wish to encourage newcomers). The payment for these services can be cash, but is often 'pick of the litter', which can mean up to fifty per cent of the litter. Unfortunately, if the supplier of the stud wishes to obtain good stock (just like you do), he will almost certainly choose the best of the litter, leaving you with the rest. For this reason, most breeders will supply this service free of charge on the understanding that, at a later unspecified date, if they need a similar service or some new young stock, you will provide these at the same rates — free! Note the earlier warning about the use of shared hobs.

If you do not know if the animals that you possess are good, bad or indifferent, then you should ask an experienced breeder for his opinion. Failing that, if you intend using your ferrets in exhibitions, carefully read the standards set out by the various ferret clubs, and compare your ferrets to these standards. However, it has to be said that reading about a subject is not as good as having first-hand experience of it. Attendance at a show will give you the opportunity of talking to experienced breeder/exhibitors about your stock and what makes a good ferret. Remember that each different variety will have a different standard for its colour and markings, but all ferrets have the same standards relating to size, type, condition, eyes and ears. Remember also that different clubs and different judges will interpret the standards slightly differently from each other, and so you should try to visit shows in other areas, rather than merely staying in your own locale.

Breeding Season

The ferret's breeding is controlled by a phenomenon known as photoperiodism; in essence this means that the animal's brain decides when the breeding season is here by the ratio of daylight hours to night-time hours. In spring, the days begin to grow longer, while the nights shorten; the opposite occurs at the onset of autumn. During the summer, the days are long, and the nights short; ambient temperatures play little part in the ferret's determination of the season.

In captivity, we can control the photoperiod (quite literally the length of light time), thus fooling our ferrets into believing that it is a different time of year than it actually is. If you are breeding animals for a business, this is essential, and the principle is used with many species, including chickens, where we need a constant supply of eggs throughout the year.

Jills will reach puberty at between five to nine months from birth and in the first 'breeding season' after their birth. Hobs reach sexual maturity a couple of months before this breeding season. As spring approaches, the female will begin to come into oestrus (season). The physical signs are self-evident, but I will explain them.

The vulva, the female's sex opening, will swell, and protrude from the body by two to three centimetres; there will also be a discharge and the jill will have a much stronger smell. As in most female mammals, at such times the jill may become irrational and bad tempered; it is not her fault, but due to a hormone imbalance. She will stay in season until mated, or to the end of the summer, although the vulva's swelling will vary from week to week. The jill is not ready for mating until the vulva has swollen fully — usually about two weeks after the first swelling occurs. Attempts to have the jill mated before this time will result in injury to the jill, and no litter.

It should be obvious that all jills kept in oestrus for any length of time will not be as happy nor as fit as they would normally be. An old country saying in the UK is that if a jill is not bred from every year, she will die at a very early age; there is a lot of truth in this, and every year many ferrets die needlessly. There is, however, no need for the jill to have a litter every year; this is explained in more detail below.

The hobs, too, change when the breeding season arrives. The hob's testicles enlarge and descend into the scrotum in the early spring and summer, allowing

A jill in season, showing her swollen vulva. If left in this condition for any length of time, she will contract oestrogen-induced anaemia, leading to leukaemia and death.

The sex organs of a hob. The testicles will not be visible in the winter, as they are withdrawn into the body.

them to breed; for the rest of the year, the testicles are out of sight, in the hob's abdomen. It is a pointless exercise trying to breed from a hob whose testicles have not descended as, even if he can perform physically, his sperm will be infertile.

When you have carefully selected the hob and jill which you wish to breed from, you can either place them both in a neutral cage, or simply put the jill in the hob's cage. Within a very short time — usually no more than a minute or so — the hob will have hold of the jill's neck, and will be dragging her to a place of his choosing; this is usually, but not necessarily, the nest-box. Once there, he will enter her, and the couple will stay tied together for two to three hours.

The actual coitus — the physical act of mating — is extremely violent and aggressive, with the hob biting the jill's neck and dragging her around the cage, mounting her several times. The whole exercise is punctuated by screams of pain from the jill, but the whole process is essential to induce ovulation.

After this mating, both ferrets will probably spend time cleaning themselves, and may even eat and drink a little. If they are left together, the hob will repeat the whole process. I have found it best to leave the pair together for no more than twenty-four hours, since more time will inevitably lead to injuries of the jill's neck. This amount of time is usually sufficient, but if you wish to be absolutely certain that the jill has been properly served, and will become pregnant, place the couple together again, about forty-eight hours later.

After the mating is completed, inspect the jill's neck, and clean the wounds, dusting them with an antiseptic powder to help guard against infection. Within seven to ten days of mating, the vulva will begin to return to normal size, and this will be complete within two to three weeks. An experienced breeder or a veterinary surgeon will be able to palpate the tummy of the jill at about ten days after the vulva is totally reduced, ie returned to its normal size.

Avoiding Unwanted Litters

In the UK and some other countries, too many ferret kits are born every year; this causes many problems and often results in what can only be described as cruel practices — abandonment of kits, euthanasia and kits going to unsuitable homes. Although one could almost forgive our ancestors of a hundred years ago for such thoughtless actions, there is no excuse for a modern ferret keeper.

As stated earlier, our ancestors recognised that jills which were not bred from each year remained in season for up to six months, and rarely lived for more than three to four years, and often much less. This is due entirely to the high levels of oestrogen — the female sex hormone — which remain in the body of the jill while she is in season; the only way to stop the build-up is for the jill to be mated. This phenomenon is known as induced ovulation, and the actual ovulation occurs about thirty hours after the mating.

If not mated, the build-up of oestrogen may well lead to a disorder known as *oestrogen-induced anaemia*, which can lead to leukaemia and the ultimate death of the jill (see chapter 9 for more details). It should be noted that it is the coitus and *not* the birth of a litter that is necessary to prevent the onset of this condition.

If you never intend breeding from your jill, the easiest way to avoid this problem is to have her neutered. However, if you may wish to have a litter in the future, as discussed in chapter 10, it is possible to treat the jill with drugs. To my mind, the easiest and best method of avoiding unwanted litters and ensuring the health of your jills is to own a hoblet — a vasectomised male.

A hoblet has merely had the tubes which transport the sperm from his testicles to his penis, cut, and so can perform exactly the same mating as a full hob. A hobble — a castrated male — has had his testicles fully removed, and so will not be capable of performing coitus at all. There is a world of difference between the two operations, but both are easily within the skills of a competent veterinary surgeon to perform.

Some ferret keepers share the services of a hoblet, but this practice is full of potential dangers, not least of all the spreading of infectious diseases among ferret kennels. If you are serious about ferrets, then you should own a hoblet.

After having been mated with a hoblet, the jill may well go into a pseudo (or phantom) pregnancy; this will last for the same length of time as a normal pregnancy (about forty-two days). At the end of this time, she may well come back into oestrus, and will require mating with a hoblet again.

The Birth of the Litter

The ferret's gestation period (pregnancy) is between forty and forty-four days, with the average being forty-two days. Where jills are kept in a commune, or several are kept together, it may be best to separate her and place her in her own cage about seven to ten days before the litter is due. This will give her time to make the cage a home, and feel comfortable and secure in it.

Many people who keep several ferrets together, leave the whole business together all year round; with some, this causes no real problems. However, where there are several ferrets in the same cage, there is always a potential for trouble among the inmates, especially during the spring and summer months.

When spring approaches, hobs and hoblets will 'come into season', and become more aggressive towards each other, with the jills, and occasionally with the handler. It is not unusual for two hobs caged together to injure each other, sometimes quite seriously. For this reason, although I have often kept the whole business together, I now invariably remove all hobs and hoblets from the courts at the onset of spring, and keep each of them in their own cage. With the jills, I treat each one as an individual; I know that some are extremely tolerant mothers, while others will not accept another jill in the same cage at breeding time. It is important that there are enough suitable cages for all the jills and hobs during the breeding season.

Once the kits are eating solids and self-sufficient, I often mix whole families, until such time as I have chosen which animals to keep, and which to let go. Even then, there may still be individuals who will not be able to tolerate each other; these must obviously be kept separately.

The signs of impending birth are obvious — nesting begins about ten days prior to the birth, and the mammary glands swell, with the nipples becoming obvious.

The Litter

Kits are born blind, deaf, naked and totally dependant on their mother, who feeds them with her own milk for the first four to six weeks of their lives, although the kits will begin eating solids from about three weeks — even before the eyes are open!

At birth, the kits weigh about eight grams, and it is important not to disturb the nest unnecessarily for at least five to seven days, although some jills, particularly the more mature ones with breeding experience, may not object or act at all adversely. When a jill feels that her litter is threatened, she acts in a way which may, to us, seem illogical; from her point of view it is perfectly logical.

When faced with the threat that a predator will kill and eat her young, the jill, who has put a lot of effort into the production of the litter, will feel like you or I would if asked to surrender our salary after having worked hard for it. She does not surrender her litter, but kills them and eats them; this turns the kits back into protein and also brings the jill back into season. This recycling of the kits helps wild polecats to ensure the continuation of the species.

Although the jill has only eight nipples, she can nurse more kits *providing that* she has sufficient food of the right type. All growing tissue requires protein, and being a parent calls for much energy, and so the jill should be provided with a high protein diet, with sufficient fats and carbohydrates for her needs. If the jill loses a

A handful of ferret kits, only two days old, and still blind, deaf and totally dependant on their mother.

The same kits in their nest.

lot of weight, it may be due to an inadequate diet, although it is quite normal for a jill to lose some weight while nursing a litter of kits.

Fostering of Kits

Very rarely, a jill cannot raise her litter; this may be due to illness or injury, or some other factor. Whatever the cause, you need to decide what you are to do with the litter. The ferret's milk is unlike cow's milk, and it is highly unlikely that you will be able raise the kits on this milk. A ferret's milk consists of 23.5% solids, of which 25.5% is protein, 34% fat, and 16.2% carbohydrate, and to successfully rear young kits, you will need to emulate this milk.

Some breeders have had a reasonable amount of luck with dog and cat milk substitutes, while I have raised ferrets from two weeks on a mixture of evaporated milk and water (1:2), mixed with the yolk of an egg. I feel that below two weeks of age, or where you cannot guarantee being able to give the one hundred and one per cent commitment to the task of hand-rearing the kits, this should not be attempted, and the kits should be humanely destroyed unless there is a viable alternative.

To help overcome such problems, and especially when the litter is extremely important, the use of a suitable foster-mother is to be recommended. I always try to have two jills giving birth on about the same day; in this way, if there is a problem with one of the jills being unable to feed part or all of her litter, I can use the other as a foster-mum. Before the kits are placed with the foster parent, she should be distracted by placing some food in her cage, well away from the nest.

To ensure that she does not simply pick up the food and carry it back to the nest immediately, give a dish of sloppy (or even liquid) food.

As she is feeding, carefully and quietly place the kits in their foster nest, and sprinkle some shavings from the cage on to them; this helps mask their smell, making them more acceptable to the foster-mother. Hopefully, the mother will return to her nest and settle down to nursing without ever realising that her litter has grown. Do not place too many foster kits with her, as this may make her incapable of looking after any of the kits properly.

Weaning

The kits develop quickly, as detailed below.

Fur erupts	9 days, profuse covering by 5 weeks
Eyes and ears open	3 — 5 weeks
Venture from nest	3 — 4 weeks
Weaning	6 — 8 weeks (about 300g — 400g)
Canine teeth erupt	7 weeks
Adult weight reached	4 months (no longer classed as kits)

Many people try to give complicated methods of weaning the kits, stating that it is essential to provide finely chopped food or even liquidised food; this is totally unnecessary, and unnatural. In the wild, the jill simply catches her normal food and carries it to the nest, where the kits help themselves; you should emulate this behaviour. The only considerations necessary are the amounts, a high protein, fat

A mother's work is never done! A jill spends much of her time dragging her kits back to their nest, which they will leave while still blind.

A three-week-old kit, with eyes just opened.

and carbohydrate content, and the removal of all uneaten food before it has a chance to go bad.

Variety to the raw meat (preferably given as whole carcasses or cadavers) is useful in ensuring a properly balanced diet, and the addition of an occasional hard boiled egg will give you a strong, healthy litter of kits destined to grow into strong, healthy ferrets.

Chapter 7

Working

As discussed in previous chapters, the ferret was probably first used by man to aid the hunting of rabbits or similar animals; today, although illegal in some countries, the practice still exists, and in the UK it is probably one of the main reasons for people to keep ferrets. It is not a sport for everyone, but it does have a lot of good points.

Rabbits are an agricultural pest which need to be controlled; many countries have laws which place responsibility for the control of rabbits and other agricultural pests on the owners and/or tenants of land, and to not control these animals is an offence against the law. When rabbits are caught by ferreting (ferrets do not fetch out the dead rabbits, and should not kill them at all), they are inevitably killed humanely and are then used as a food source, either for humans, animals or both. To my mind, this makes the practice incredibly 'green', since not only are we controlling pest species, we are also providing good healthy meat. While alive, the rabbits live a perfectly natural life, and are not subjected to many of the excesses that domestic food species suffer in captivity.

Public enemy No.1! The rabbit is an agricultural pest and, although difficult to see, can easily be scented and hunted by mustelids such as the ferret.

Rabbit holes dug under buildings; rabbits can cause great damage to farm buildings, and their numbers must be controlled

The rat is another species which has been successfully hunted and controlled by using ferrets, although the cadavers of such sport cannot be eaten, due to the risk of disease. Ferrets used for ratting need to be smaller than those used for rabbiting, and should have gained at least two years' experience against rabbits before being used on the rat — a far fiercer adversary. One of the biggest dangers facing those who hunt rats is Weil's Disease, or leptospirosis (sometimes called leptospiral jaundice), commonly known as the 'Rat Catcher's Yellows'. This is caused by spirochaetes, a type of bacteria and, in common with other bacteria, once this enters your blood stream (perhaps through a cut or graze on the hand), it causes a fever and produces toxic substances, often with fatal results.

These bacteria do not affect the host animal, the rat, which is therefore known as a passive carrier, and it is thought that the rat and the spirochaetes may have evolved together, since the bacteria require a host animal in which they can survive and which they do not damage, in order that the bacteria themselves are not wiped out. Some of the bacteria are passed out in the rat's urine and all that is needed is for a human to get some of that urine on a cut or graze, and he is infected. Likewise, eating food with hands soiled with rat urine is a sure way of infecting one's body with these bacteria.

The first symptoms — fever, diarrhoea, severe thigh pains and vomiting — appear within a few days of the infection, and within a week the victim is jaundiced, owing to liver damage. It is usually at this stage that the family doctor is given some indication of the nature of the illness and, if he is to treat the patient successfully, he must move quickly, since if he does not, and the patient's own immune system is not too strong, the patient may be dead within the next seven to ten days.

This information is not intended to frighten the reader, merely to inform him of the possible dangers of hunting the rat. These dangers can be minimised by wearing strong rubber gloves when hunting rats and by adhering to a strict hygiene routine, ie always washing hands well before eating or drinking. Ferrets used for ratting will inevitably get infected urine on them at some time, and by handling these ferrets, you may well infect yourself. Ferrets cannot catch Weil's Disease.

Obtaining Hunting Permission

Whichever quarry you decide to hunt, you must obtain permission from the person who is legally entitled to grant it to you; this varies from country to country, and so the reader should check with a legal expert if he is in any doubt about who can grant such permission.

I have found the best way to get hunting permission is to keep a lookout for areas where there is a definite problem with, say, rabbits. Next, ascertain who owns or leases the land, and contact him by telephone to make mutually convenient arrangements to visit him. When you go, do not wear your ferreting clothes, but go along in a respectable outfit; first impressions count!

Explain to the landowner that you believe he has a rabbit problem and that you would like his permission to reduce the rabbit population with your ferrets. In return, you will supply him with some of the dead rabbits, and will respect his property. Don't be too disappointed if you have several unsuccessful meetings before you get your big break. However, once you are given the chance, do the job well, be courteous and always offer the man a couple of rabbits from each trip. News of a good and efficient rabbit controller travels fast, and you will probably get more offers of ferreting. This is how I started, and today I have more ferreting than I can handle on a regular basis.

Starting Out

The amount of equipment needed for hunting rabbits with ferrets is minimal — ferrets and nets are sufficient, although, as we shall see, some other items of equipment will help us be more efficient and effective.

The ferrets chosen for hunting should be of average size; too big and they cannot manoeuvre enough; too small and they will not possess the reserves of energy needed for a full day's working. The colour of working ferrets causes arguments and discussion among many ferreters, with strong opinions being expressed in all directions by the parties concerned. The adherents of the white ferrets will tell you that it is easier to see the ferret when it leaves the burrow, although as much ferreting takes place in the winter months, when the snow is on the ground, this argument is not too sound. On the other hand, the adherents of the poley will tell you that these darker coloured animals are keener to hunt and much more ferocious, making them the better colour for hunting purposes – an equally fallacious argument.

Similar arguments exist where ferrets are used in conjunction with hawks. Some *austringers* (those who hunt with hawks) will tell you that white ferrets must never be used, as they resemble the colour of the day-old chicks fed to the hawks, while others will tell you that only white ferrets should be used, so that the hawk will not think the ferret is a rabbit.

None of these arguments are true. My own theory for these tales is that, when the story teller obtained their first ferret, they had no choice of colour, and now seek ways to justify their 'choice'. I have never noticed any real difference in the working abilities of ferrets which can be linked to the colour of their fur; if a ferret works well, it is the right one for the job, regardless of its colour and markings.

Another argument which rages with rabbiting ferreters is that regarding which sex is best. Many hunters will not use (or even keep) hobs, saying that they are useless for work; these people hunt only jills. Some say that most jills are too small to be able to work for long enough periods, and so only use hobs. It is true to say that the great majority of ferreters use mainly jills, with hobs only being used for specialised roles, such as a 'liner' (see below for more details). I must state here that one of the very best working ferrets that I have ever possessed was a hob which was rescued from a man who no longer wanted his ferrets; the hob worked long and hard, would not go underground if there were no rabbits in the burrow, and would not come out until his job was done. I was very sad when he was stolen from me (along with ten other ferrets) in February 1994.

The basic concept in ferreting rabbits is to find a burrow occupied by rabbits, and then introduce one or more ferrets into that burrow. It is best to work with at least two ferrets, as rabbits in a large burrow can easily give a single ferret the run-around. We hope that the ferret will not actually catch any rabbits, merely flush them out for us to deal with (although I'm sure that the ferrets have other ideas!). The ferret is aided in this endeavour by its smell, and old timers used to attach bells to the ferret's collar to scare the rabbits, and also to aid in finding the ferret.

Types of Rabbiting

There are four main methods of catching rabbits flushed from their holes by ferrets — nets, guns, hawks and dogs; by far the most commonly practised method employs nets.

There are two main types of net used — purse-nets and long-nets. Purse-nets are placed over every hole, to catch the rabbits as they flee the burrow, while long-nets (at least when used for ferreting) are placed around the whole burrow, to catch the rabbits as they try to escape from the area. The two complement each other, and are best employed together, as it is all too easy to miss an opening to the burrow, and the fleeing rabbit can then be caught up in the long-net. Even where a purse-net is correctly set over a hole, it is not impossible for a rabbit to escape from it and, without the back-up provided by the long-net, the rabbits would escape to cause problems in another burrow. It may seem like a case of using both belt and braces, but better safe than sorry!

A correctly set purse-net. These nets are useless if set incorrectly, and the art must be learned over many outings.

A long-net, set around a rabbit bury in order to catch any rabbits who escape the purse-nets set on all (hopefully!) of the holes leading to the rabbit burrow.

Where sport, and not the actual number of rabbits caught, is the main priority, ferrets are simply entered into the burrow and the fleeing rabbits shot by carefully placed Guns. This method will not result in the numbers caught by using nets, as the noise of the shots will dissuade many, though by no means all, rabbits from bolting. It is also essential that all Guns (ie those people actually shooting at the rabbits) are one hundred per cent safe, and no shots are taken which may put at risk any human, ferret, dog or indeed any animal other than the quarry — the rabbits.

Using hawks to catch rabbits will give even smaller bags, but excellent sport. I do not intend to give the full details of hawking here, as it is a sport and subject in itself. Many books have been written on the subject, and these should be read and digested, and the guidance of experienced *austringers* sought by readers who wish to find out more about this fascinating sport. The main principles in this sport are to have a suitably trained species of hawk, such as the Harris hawk (*Parabuteo unicinctus*), which is held on the fist until the ferret flushes a rabbit from the burrow. The hawk is then released and catches the rabbit.

Many varieties of dog are used for hunting rabbits in conjunction with ferrets, and all have their adherents. Again, I can only skim over the subject in this book, as our main concern is the ferret; again I recommend that interested readers consult practitioners and books for further information.

In essence, there are two main types of dog used for catching the rabbits flushed by our ferrets — gaze hounds and terriers. Gaze hounds, or lurchers, hunt their quarry by sight and need open space to be successful; they work well where one is ferreting a bank on the edge of open fields. Terriers do not have such a turn of speed, but are

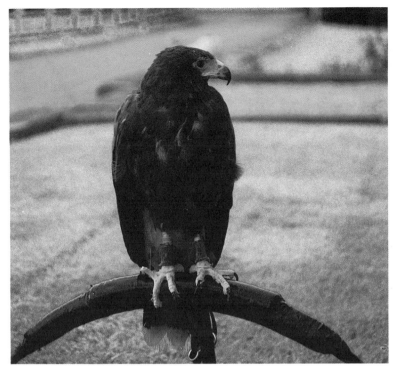

A Harris hawk, one of the most popular raptors employed with ferrets.

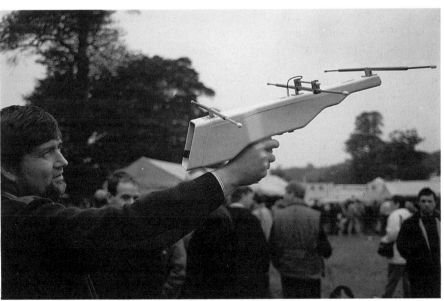

An electronic device for tracking hawks equipped with a matching transmitter. The author believes that it is in everyone's interest that all hawks used in hunting are fitted with such a device.

much more manoeuvrable than lurchers, and can work well in undergrowth where lurchers could not operate. Both types of dog, however, have a use which any ferreter will appreciate; they can be trained to mark burrows which contain rabbits, thus eliminating time wasted by netting up and entering ferrets into empty burrows.

Training

A lot has been written about the need to train a ferret to do its job correctly, ie to hunt rabbits. Some books devote huge sections to this aspect of ferreting. To my mind, there is no need to teach an animal to carry out a perfectly natural function. The ferret is, by nature, a predator — a hunting animal — and, left to its own devices, it will do the job naturally. Undoubtedly, the best way for a young ferret to learn its trade is to follow the example of an experienced ferret but, if you do not possess such an animal, do not despair!

Most animals have an instinctive fear of the unknown and, for this reason, some young ferrets may be reluctant to enter a dark tunnel which heads down almost vertically. Choose instead, a reasonable size tunnel in a burrow that you know is uninhabited and consists of no more than two or three holes. Ensure that the tunnel, initially at least, slopes slightly upwards and place the ferret just in the mouth of the tunnel. Do not worry if she pauses and sniffs the air for a time before venturing into the abyss, this is perfectly natural. Do not try to force her underground before she is ready; to do so may cause the ferret to fear the underground world, thus rendering it virtually useless for hunting. Patience will pay dividends!

After one or two outings of this nature, take the tyro to a small burrow where you would expect to find a rabbit or two and enter her. Once she has had her first encounter with the cast of *Watership Downs*, there will be no stopping her! Remember that she will be very excited when she comes out of the hole, and so do not try to pick her up before she has completely left the hole. To do so will encourage her to 'skulk', ie always wait just inside the entrance to a tunnel and move away from your hand every time that you try to pick her up. It is easier to start this habit than it is to stop it!

By the time that your ferret has been entered to occupied rabbit holes a few times, it will be fully 'trained' and, in future, whenever you take the ferret out of its cage to put it into its carrying-box, she will realise that she is probably going hunting, and may even tremble with excitement. This excitement will always be evident when the ferret is taken out of the carrying-box on site, and introduced to the opening in the ground from which exudes the unmistakable aroma of rabbit! Your ferrets will look forward to such outings and consider them in exactly the same way that we do — not work but good, clean fun with (hopefully) a good meal of rabbit flesh at the end of the day!

With experience, ferrets will learn which burrows are occupied; I have had many ferrets which simply refuse to go into some burrows (presumably because there are no rabbits in them), and yet will dash into others with much gusto and enthusiasm. Rabbits are inevitably caught from burrows where the ferrets act in the latter manner.

Ferreted rabbits lodged in a tree to cool. It is vital that such action is taken as soon after death as possible, to ensure good quality meat.

Equipment

Ferrets

The number of ferrets required will be determined by the area to be worked and, of course, by the number you have available. As stated earlier, I will never attempt any bury with less than two ferrets; if a liner is to be used, this figure would obviously be three. In large warrens, I like to take along at least two pairs of free working jills plus a hob that I can use as a liner. In a very large warren, the two teams may be worked together, but I usually alternate one team with the other throughout the day.

Many modern ferreters do not use a liner, and I believe this to be to the detriment of the sport. A liner is simply a hob ferret which is kept separate from all other ferrets, and so does not get on with them. He is used when a free-working ferret 'kills-down' and then 'lays-up', ie refuses to leave the dead rabbit, or when a ferret is trapped, either by a collapsed roof or some other obstacle. His job is to seek out the kill, and then chase away the errant ferret, while he stays next to the dead rabbit. The old fashioned method was to attach line to his collar, via a swivel. The other end of the line is held by the ferreter, and as the line is marked every metre, he will be able to calculate how far into the burrow the liner is. Since the introduction of electronic detectors, few ferreters have bothered to learn how to use such an animal, which is a great pity since, no matter how good modern gadgets are, they can — and do! — fail, and it is then that a good, reliable and efficient back-up is needed.

I will confess, however, that the way that I usually use a liner is not the traditional way. If I have a lay-up, I use a hob as above but, instead of fitting him with a line, which all too frequently snags on underground roots and other such obstacles, I fit him with an electronic transmitter attached to his collar. He does exactly the same job, ie he finds the errant free-working jill and/or the dead rabbit and, after having chased off the jill, he curls up at the side of the kill to await my digging him out. The advantages of using this modern method of lining are many, including the almost total lack of ferrets getting caught on underground roots etc, and the ability to check his location while digging him out; many ferrets which have refused to budge for hours, will move the instant that they hear you digging for them. With practice, this method can save many hours of hard digging — a positive advantage!

Carrying-boxes
The ferrets used for the hunting trips must, of course, be transported to and from the working area and I believe they deserve to travel in comfort. I do not like the carrying bags or sacks which are favoured by some, as they give the ferrets very little protection form the cold and wet, and no protection at all from clumsy feet! A good carrying-box made from plywood, and measuring about 45cm x 25cm x 25cm high, is a far better method of transporting ferrets. It should be of stout construction, while remaining reasonably light, and also be weather-proof. The addition of a couple of small drainage holes in the bottom will help keep the inside reasonably clean and dry, and I find it beneficial to have two completely separate compartments, enabling me to select which ferrets to use, while preventing the others from escaping. I prefer to have a separate door on each compartment, rather than a sliding door which always allows one side to be open.

A selection of carrying-boxes suitable for working ferrets. These are to be preferred to bags which, in the author's opinion, should never be used.

Adequate ventilation holes must be provided in each compartment, since even in winter, fresh air is essential for the well-being of the ferrets. Place an ample quantity of wood shavings and hay in the bottom of each compartment; this will help absorb moisture, thus keeping the ferrets dry and comfortable, to keep them warm and also prevent them from being knocked around too much in transit.

The box should have a broad, strong carrying strap for ease of use; make sure that the strap is properly secured to the box and is the correct length to ensure reasonable comfort for you whilst carrying the box. You will find that when you need to climb over obstacles, a single strap will come off your shoulder; this is very annoying and dangerous for both you and your ferrets. Twin straps, such as fitted on rucksacks, will help prevent this.

Electronic Detector

I first started to use an electronic 'ferret detector' in 1978, and have never looked back. Used correctly and with care, these gadgets save much time and hard work, and help to ensure that all killed rabbits are found. The device consists of a pre-tuned receiver and a collar mounted transmitter, each with replaceable batteries which are light and give many hours of use. Although quite expensive, they do last for many years, if looked after and properly maintained, and I would recommend them to any serious ferreter.

An electronic ferret locator in a leather case with (top to bottom) micro, standard, and 15' collars.

Only one receiver is required, but each ferret should be equipped with a collar when working underground. Before entering a ferret wearing such a collar, wrap a piece of plastic insulating tape around both the transmitter — to secure the fastening — and the loose end of the collar; the latter will help minimise the risks of the trailing tip of the collar becoming snagged and/or the collar coming off completely.

Some ferreters prefer to use their free-working ferrets without transmitters and, instead, utilise a liner fitted with one, as detailed before. I like to use all of my ferrets with radio transmitter collars attached, thereby keeping me in touch with all of the subterranean happenings.

After use, all batteries should be removed from the transmitter and the collars, and their attachments thoroughly cleaned and dried, prior to storage. Never store the transmitters or receivers with their batteries still in place, as leakage can occur and cause damage. In use, the receiver must be held upright and swung about thirty centimetres above the ground where the ferret is thought to be. To make life easier, I attach a length of cord to my receiver, enabling me to swing it very close to the ground without having to walk in a stoop.

Once the detector picks up the signal from the ferret's collar transmitter, the receiver will start to make a noise, usually a loud and rapid ticking. When this noise is heard, move more carefully until you have narrowed the area down to about one metre square. By adjusting the control on the receiver, you will reduce the sensitivity of the detector and so, by carefully moving the receiver and reducing its sensitivity, it is possible to track a ferret while it is working underground and, when it stops, to find its position to within about five to ten centimetres. Practice makes perfect!

Insulation Tape

Good quality plastic insulation tape has many uses on a ferreting day, including those outlined above, and a roll should always be carried. The terminals of spare batteries can be protected against the possibility of short circuits by pieces of this material, and loose ends of collars, belts and straps secured to prevent them from snagging.

Spade, Chad or Graft

Although I always hope that I will not need to dig, I always take the precaution of including a suitable spade in my equipment — just in case! The traditional tool for digging out is called a 'chad' or 'graft', but any small bladed spade of strong, top quality construction will do the job. Post diggers, used by many navvies during their work, are ideal and can often be obtained for a small cost.

In some English counties, grafts were designed and constructed for use by professional rabbiters and warreners; the most famous of these is the Norfolk long-graft, known in its native county as a Norfolk paddle. It is a huge instrument, measuring about 250cm from one end to the other. The blade is pointed, like a spade, but dished and cranked, like a shovel. This makes it easy to break through hard soil, and then lift it out of the burrow on the blade. At the top of the handle is a hook; this was used to lift out the liner, by sliding the hook under his collar, or twisting his line around the

A selection of ferreting spades or 'grafts'. The second one from the left is a 'Norfolk Long-graft', specifically designed and manufactured in Norfolk, UK, for use by professional warreners. This particular model, with an eight-foot (250cm) shaft and narrow blade, is designed for use in hard soil, and is referred to by locals as a 'paddle'. For sandy soils, a more dished graft — called a 'spoon' — was used. This type of graft takes some getting used to; the author prefers the American style (on left) for soft and sandy soils, and a small-bladed spade for hard digging.

hook. Some warreners used to sharpen the hook, which could then be used to skewer the dead rabbit from the burrow.

Whichever design you decide on, it must be fit for its task, and needs to be strong enough to last for many years. All good quality tools are expensive and skimping on these is courting disaster. After use, clean the whole instrument and wipe the blade with an oily rag to help prevent corrosion.

Mink Trap

This is an important part of ferreting equipment, often neglected by newcomers to the sport. Such a trap, designed to catch mink and similar animals alive, should always be taken along on ferreting trips. Should a ferret be lost underground and you need to leave the area without having recaptured it, the trap can be left to do its work while you are fast asleep in your bed. When a ferret is lost down a burrow, and all efforts to retrieve it have failed, set the trap, using a piece of rabbit for bait, and place it near to the entrance of the burrow where the ferret was last seen. Carefully cover the top and sides, thus giving the animal shelter when caught in the trap, and then leave it. All such traps must be inspected every few hours, in case a ferret has been caught.

If you do not have such a trap with you, digging a pit, which should be baited with rabbit, or leaving the ferret's carrying box near the burrow may also work. You should not easily abandon any ferret; in many countries this is illegal, and in any case it is certainly immoral.

Milk

Ferrets will become tired and thirsty after working, in exactly the same way that we do; they deserve to be given a little light refreshment. A small container of milk and a small dish in your equipment bag will enable the ferrets to enjoy a 'tea-break' while you have yours. A light snack of rabbit meat will also be welcomed!

Purse-nets

The use of these has already been discussed. They are nets which are placed over the entrance/exit holes to the bury, into which the rabbits will bolt; they get their name from the fact that they are designed on the same principle as the old-fashioned draw-stringed purse, and are traditionally made from hemp, although most today are made from nylon and other man-made fibres. You will never have too many.

Although the construction varies only in quality, it is worth shopping around to obtain the best quality nets that you can. Colour does not matter; I have used nets dyed red, blue, yellow, green, brown, black and many other colours — all with varying degrees of success. The most important aspect of purse-nets is their setting — do it wrongly and no net, regardless of colour, will rectify your mistakes.

There are advantages and disadvantages with nets made from both natural and man-made materials. Hemp, if stored while still damp, rots; nylon does not. Nylon slips very easily, making it unsuitable for some applications, hemp does not. Hemp nets are relatively expensive when compared to those made from nylon. I use nets made from both types of material, and of differing sizes; only experience can teach you which are best for you in specific circumstances.

All purse-nets must be well made, utilising two good quality rings. Whatever the material it must be top quality, with the mesh big enough to allow an adult ferret to pass through easily, while preventing a rabbit from doing the same. A knot to knot size of about five to six centimetres is generally accepted as the correct size of mesh. Around the neck of the purse-net is the draw-string, which actually purses the net when a rabbit hits it. This draw-string must be strong and the ends securely tied to a peg. If using nylon for the draw-strings, utilise a double fisherman's knot.

The pegs that hold the net into the ground are traditionally made from well-seasoned hazel, sharpened at one end and a hole drilled though the other end through which the draw-string is fastened. The sheer cost of these items means that many ferreters use other types of wood for the pegs. Where the ground is extremely hard, for instance in times of prolonged and heavy frosts, I often use metal pegs, such as meat skewers or tent-pegs. During transit, nets must be folded in such a way that they are easy to deploy and, after use, they should be cleaned thoroughly and allowed to dry before being put into storage, particularly in the case of hemp nets.

All nets — purse and long — can be home-made, providing that one has the requisite time, patience and skill. While this can undoubtedly save money, I prefer to buy them, saving my spare time for actual ferreting.

Long-nets

Long-nets are also made from either hemp or nylon, and their use has been described earlier in this chapter. The standard length for a modern long-net is one hundred metres, although many that were made some years ago will be one hundred yards, and they can also be bought in twenty-five and fifty metre lengths. Several nets are often joined together to produce netting for a particular use. To support the long-nets, stakes are required, and again the traditional material is well-seasoned hazel. Ensure that they are given a good point to ease their fixing in the ground, which is often rock hard. The use of long-nets takes much experience and skill, and if the reader is interested, the help of an experienced practitioner should be sought.

Knives

Both a sheath and a lock-knife should be carried on hunting trips; the sheath knife used for hacking away foliage or cutting branches to use as probes, and the lock-knife for gutting the rabbits. Ensure that both knives are kept sharp, as a blunt blade is worse than useless.

Collars and Line

Collars for liners should be made of best quality soft leather, kept supple by the use of a proprietary saddle-soap or leather treatment. The line should be of nylon, and at least ten metres long, attached to the collar via a good quality swivel. To help you gauge how far the liner has travelled underground, mark the line with a waterproof ink mark every metre. Never mark the line by tying knots in it, as these cause problems by constantly snagging on every underground obstacle.

| *A probe, or proggling stick, used to track the rabbits' tunnels.* | *The business end of the probe, showing the enlarged piece a few centimetres above the point. It is this bulge which produces an over-sized hole, and allows the operator to know when he breaks through into the tunnel.* |

Probe

This is another traditional piece of equipment that has fallen into obscurity. It is a blunt-ended metal (usually iron) rod with a small bulge about one hundred centimetres from the point. It is used to trace the path of a tunnel by pushing it into the ground and feeling for lack of resistance. Even though it has a blunt point to protect the ferret, it can still injure them if used too harshly, and so great care must be taken in its use.

Clothing

Clothing used for ferreting needs to be robust, strong and able to protect the wearer from the rigours of the weather and natural obstacles such as thorns. All clothing must be roomy enough to allow free movement, without causing discomfort, and outer garments are best if windproof and preferably waterproof.

Clothes worn during a ferreting expedition have a nasty habit of becoming very wet, dirty and smelly, and so it is advisable to have a complete change of clothing and footwear in the car, along with a couple of towels for drying yourself. A large plastic bag will be useful to place dirty clothing in.

Do not make the mistake of believing that an accumulation of equipment will help you be better at ferreting; many of the best ferreters use only a minimal amount of gear. Knowledge and experience, neither of which can be bought, are the two essentials for good sport and effective rabbit clearance.

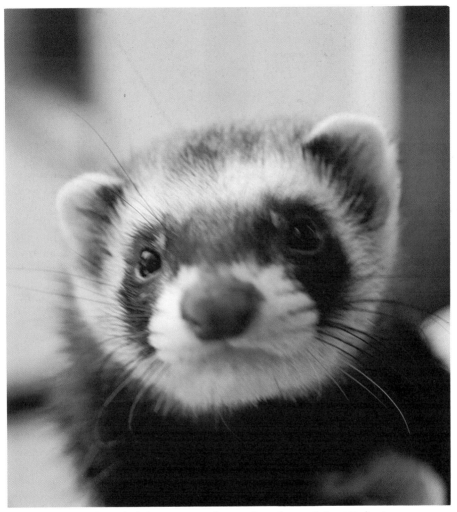

A polecat hob in summer pelage, when the mask is at its best.

Chapter 8

Showing, Racing and Pets

Although ferrets have been used for thousands of years for hunting purposes, many of today's owners prefer to have them as 'fancy' animals, ie for exhibition purposes, for shows or simply as pets. Decried by some, welcomed with tremendous enthusiasm by others, these alternative uses for ferrets have made the animal even more popular and, in some countries, are the only reasons for possessing ferrets, as hunting with them is either banned or incredibly difficult to obtain permission for.

The Fancy

Ferret shows are today popular around the world, and it has proven impossible for me to discover when the first 'official' ferret show took place. However, I know that back in the 1970s small shows were regularly being staged in the UK, as I was often asked to judge at them. They were small, low-key affairs, and those taking part looked on them as harmless fun. Today, with so many people showing as their *raison d'être*, some take the subject very seriously indeed. There is nothing wrong with this, as long as the well-being of the ferrets is always put first, and any hobby needs to be fun or it soon becomes work.

Throughout the world, people have sat down and described their ideas of the perfect ferret; this is usually very subjective, rather than objective, and varies enormously between countries, regions, clubs and even individuals. If you are intent on being successful at showing, you should carefully study the standards for your area, and your animals must comply with them if you are to stand a chance of winning.

My worry in all of this is that the ferret fancy may go the way of the dog fancy; the standards for many dogs are exaggerated, and the animals themselves are often put at physical risk because of this. Some breeds of dog are bred with heads so large that they cannot give birth normally, and have to endure an elective Caesarean section; others are bred with such short noses that they have difficulty breathing. Some standards call for animals with such fine bones that, when the animal behaves at all naturally, they are in danger of breaking those bones, while others have so much wrinkled flesh on their faces that their eyesight suffers.

To my mind, we should set standards for the ferret which encourage breeders to produce animals which are entirely normal — capable of full working lives, and able to exist without any interference from man, if need be. This would seem to be common sense, but as we have seen, this seems to be sadly lacking in many fancies. Even today, many in the ferret fancy are breeding animals with exaggerated physical characteristics. I have witnessed many ferrets — both hobs and jills — which are twice the size of the normal animal; their heads are so big and broad that I am sure some complications must occur at birth. Please let common sense prevail, for the ferret's sake!

I have here set out a few principles that I hope clubs will base their standards on; I have not set hard and fast rules, simply commonsense considerations, which are in the best interests of the ferret. The terminology used in fancy animals also needs a little explanation, and again I have given a few guide-lines.

The categories under which points are allotted are;

> Colour and markings
> Type
> Fur
> Size
> Condition
> Eyes and ears

The first category, colour and markings, is the one which has most variance, and so I will not say anything on this except to suggest that, in patterned varieties fifty per cent of the points for this category should be allocated for colour and markings and fifty per cent for pattern. I also feel that for shows to be successful, different colours should be judged in separate classes, with the overall results coming from the result of the comparison of each animal against its standard, and *not* each other.

'Type', or configuration as it is sometimes called, refers to the overall shape of the ferret. The ferret should have a long, lean body, which arches when the animal is at rest, with short legs; its gait should be easy and effortless. The tail should be about half as long as the body. The head should be proportionate to the body, with the hob having a much broader skull; the face of the animal may be pointed or blunt, as neither are detrimental to the animal. The head should be well set into the body, the profile showing a smooth curve from nose over head to nape of neck. The neck should be cylindrical, and noticeably long, blending gradually with the slender and elongated thorax and abdomen.

The fur should be soft and very dense, with due allowances made for animals which have been neutered (this tends to give them a better coat). The coat should consist of fine underfur and longer, more coarse guard hairs, and the tail should be well furred.

The ferret should be lean, not fat, and of a size which would allow the animal to lead a normal predatory life. Allowance should be made for sex, ie hobs are larger than jills.

The ferret should be fit, curious when well-awake, and tame to handle. The flesh should be firm with no surplus fat, and the coat have a healthy sheen, with the ferret being quite clean.

The eyes should be small and widely set with the ears being small and discreet, set well apart on the head.

The teeth should be white and the ferret should have a complete set. The jaws should meet correctly.

Penalties should be incurred for the following reasons;

     Intractability
     Disease or injury
     Excess fat
     Sores, wounds or scars
     Dirty fur
     Missing limb, eye, ear, foot or tail
     Any deformity believed by the judge to be hereditary
     Under/over-shot jaws
     Damaged or missing teeth

No penalties should be incurred by ferrets with a slight amount of wax in their ears. This is perfectly normal and is actually an aid to the ferret's well-being. Where the ears have been scrubbed out, and may even show signs of irritation from the process, penalties should be incurred.

Ferret Racing

This is a sport that started in the USA and has proven popular in many countries, particularly the United Kingdom, where such events feature strongly at most country fairs and similar events. When properly organised, the crowds find the spectacle fascinating, and the ferrets seem to enjoy themselves.

The legend surrounding the invention of this sport is that oil workers used ferrets to pass lines through pipelines; once through, the lines could be attached to cameras, welding machinery etc, which could then be hauled through the pipe. At night, with very little to do, the workers would take bets on the fastest ferret to go through a length of pipe.

When the idea arrived in the UK, it was suitably tweaked to allow for British conditions. Today, the average ferret race takes place between six ferrets, who have to run down identical lengths of piping (all of the same bore). At intervals along the pipes, gaps are left (to help the public see where the ferrets are), and the trick is to encourage the ferret to ignore them and continue to the end of the piping.

Again, the potential problems are that some breeders will develop lines of ferrets which are very small and fast, to enable the animals to complete the course at high speed; the danger is that these animals will be too small and fast to allow them to lead a predatory life, ie they will become unnatural.

***

Whatever the sport, while the ferrets are waiting to be judged or raced, the organisers should arrange suitable holding facilities, where the ferrets can be rested, fed, watered and exercised, and that area should have shelter from prevailing temperatures and weather conditions. (See Appendix 5).

Pets

As a pet, the ferret leaves most of its competitors in the shade. Despite the unwarranted bad reputation that the ferret has for being aggressive and biting needlessly and indiscriminately, ferrets are actually very easily tameable, and with regular careful handling can be handled with total safety by all but the smallest child.

Their size means that they can take a reasonable amount of fairly rough handling, and can also be taken for walks on a lead, as a small dog or cat would be. Guaranteed to turn heads as they walk down the street on a harness and leash, the ferrets really seem to enjoy their airing and the chance to see so many happenings that they would not normally witness.

Many people keep ferrets in the house, giving them complete freedom to wander around; when questioned on this, the owners simply state that it is no different to a cat or dog having free reign in the human home! Ferrets do, however, have the knack of getting into all the wrong places. I have heard of ferrets which nest in the bottoms of cookers, in drawers of underwear, and even in human beds!

If your ferret is allowed free access around the home, ensure that all visitors are made aware of this, and watch where everyone puts their feet, since a booted foot can cause serious injury to a ferret. Every room should be equipped with a litter tray, which will need to be emptied and cleaned regularly, and food and water dishes should also be routinely serviced. Don't forget that ferrets like to hide their food around their home, and so you shouldn't be surprised if you find a half-eaten chunk of meat tucked away inside your favourite shoe!

Transport

Whatever your reason for having ferrets, you will need some sort of carrier to transport the animals, whether it be to a show, a race, the vet, or simply on your holiday. The choice of a suitable carrier should be given some thought and different types will appeal to different people.

Perhaps the most popular type of carrier is that sold in pet shops for cats and other small animals. Made from high impact plastic or polycarbonate, they have a door which swings open at the front, and a carrying handle on top. They are also made in such a way as to allow the top to be completely separated from the bottom, and this makes cleaning easy.

Many people use wooden boxes, and these are adequate if one remembers that wood is porous, and so is difficult to keep scrupulously clean, and needs to have regular attention to prevent the ferret's urine soaking into the wood with the resultant smell and rotting. Regular treatment of the box with a safe wood preserver will help give the box a long working life.

Some ferret owners like baskets; I do not. They are insanitary, being impossible to keep clean, and draughty for the animals.

Whatever type of container you use for transporting your ferrets, ensure that they have adequate ventilation, and never leave them in the sun, or in a closed car, as the heat can rise to a lethal temperature very quickly.

Bathing

Although not generally in favour of bathing ferrets on a regular basis, I recognise that there are times when a ferret requires a bath. He may have become soiled while being transported, he may be ill or have an infestation of ectoparasites, or you may be ensuring that he looks his best before placing him on the show bench.

Shampoos designed for use on cats are ideal for ferrets; use of an insecticidal shampoo, even if your ferret does not have fleas, will act as a preventative measure and is to be recommended.

Use a bowl specifically for the ferret; using the same bowl that you wash your clothes or even dinner pots in is extremely insanitary and a crass habit. Run a small amount (about 4cm - 5cm) of tepid water into the bottom of the bowl, and place a mat or piece of cloth in it. This will help the ferret to obtain a purchase, preventing him slipping around, and therefore panicking. Next, carefully place the ferret in the bowl, talking softly to him the whole time.

When he is reasonably happy, remembering that repetition will aid his acceptance of this, gently pour some of the tepid water over him, working it into the fur all the way down to the base; avoid the eyes and ears. Next, pour a little shampoo on his fur and gently massage it well into the coat, again avoiding the eyes and ears. When he is covered with a good lather, and the shampoo has been worked well down into the coat, rinse with fresh tepid water. Repeat this procedure, ensuring that the ferret's coat is well rinsed of all remains of the shampoo.

Lift the ferret gently from the bowl and wrap in a towel; again this should be one used solely for the ferret. Rub him vigorously, removing most of the water, and then place him in an open fronted cage out of draughts. Position a hair dryer, or electric fan heater, about twenty centimetres from the front of the cage, and switch it on to low, directing the stream of warm air into the cage. Keep a careful check on the ferret and, within about five to ten minutes, he should be dry and can be removed from the cage. Never return a damp ferret to an unheated cage area, or one that is out-of-doors, regardless of the ambient temperature or prevailing weather conditions.

If the ears are very dirty, dip a cotton bud into warmed olive oil, and gently wipe the pinnae (ear flaps) one at a time, using a separate cotton bud for each ear. Once completed, use a fresh, dry bud to remove the debris. *Never* push the bud into the ear, nor should you use undue force or a scrubbing motion.

If you fear that your ferret has ear mites, consult your veterinary surgeon, who will prescribe specific ear-drops.

Chapter 9

Ailments and First Aid

Properly cared for, the ferret is an extremely healthy and hardy animal, and many owners have never experienced serious medical problems with any of their ferrets. However, accidents can and do happen, and illness is certainly not unknown among ferrets. Unfortunately, ferrets are still very much 'wild animals' and as such, tend to mask symptoms of illness — often until it is too late to help them. Any unusual behaviour among your ferrets should have you checking more vigilantly, and no veterinary surgeon will mind being consulted for an animal which is not at death's door.

In many countries, ferrets are so cheap that vets rarely see any in their surgery; it is cheaper and easier for uncaring owners to kill the luckless ferret than to have it treated. As more people are attracted to ferrets, and more knowledge is gained about all aspects of the animal, this sad state of affairs will hopefully come to an end.

The Basics of First Aid

The old saying that things are as easy as A B C is very true when it comes to first-aid, the ABC being — AIRWAYS, BREATHING, CIRCULATION. In other words, if the patient is not breathing, get the airways clear before you try to get the animal breathing, and only once the animal is breathing should you concern yourself with the heart and/or bleeding.

All first-aid principles are the same, regardless of species involved, and I cannot recommend too highly that everyone should have a basic training in the subject. Such organisations as the Red Cross and the St. John Ambulance Service run courses at very reasonable rates, and going on one may help you save a life!

I have found two widely used definitions which I feel help to explain the subject;

'First-aid is the skilled application of accepted principles of treatment, on the occurrence of an accident, or in the case of a sudden illness, using facilities and materials available at the time.'

'First-aid is the approved method of treating a casualty until they are placed, if necessary, in the care of a qualified medical practitioner, or removed to a hospital.'

The objects of first-aid are three-fold — to sustain life, to prevent the patient's condition worsening and to promote the patient's recovery. The methods used are;

    a Assess the situation;
    b Diagnose the condition;
    c Treat immediately and adequately.

Remember to ensure your own safety at all times.

Prevention is, of course, better than cure. Ensure that your ferrets are given a good, balanced diet; their cages cleaned regularly; they are not subjected to extremes of temperatures; are kept away from draughts, and are not stressed unnecessarily. Any cuts, abrasions or bites must be cleaned and treated immediately.

First Aid

Some of the most common ferret injuries — minor cuts and abrasions — occur when the animal is going about its daily routine, or is being worked, and it is important that they are treated as soon as possible in order to minimise adverse effects on the animal. In order to do this, a small first-aid kit should be taken along on every hunting foray and, of course, you should have the necessary skill and experience to treat these minor injuries; if there is any doubt as to the seriousness of the injuries, or the ferret's general condition, veterinary treatment should be sought as soon as practical.

A suitable first-aid kit for ferrets should contain the following items as a minimum, and should always accompany you on any field trip and be near at hand at all times.

1. Nail clippers
These should be top quality and can be used for trimming the ferret's nails. Use the type which work on the guillotine principle, where one blade hits the other, rather than on the scissor principle which can result in nails being pulled out. Ferrets' nails should not be cut too short; leave about 5mm beyond the quick.

2. Tweezers
For the removal of foreign bodies.

3. Scissors
These should be curved and round ended and are to be used to cut off the fur around any wound. They must *not* be used for trimming nails.

4. Antiseptic lotion
For cleansing cuts, wounds and abrasions.

5. Antibiotic powder
Should be applied to wounds after they have been thoroughly cleansed. This powder is only available from a veterinary surgeon who will only supply it after he has seen the wound in question.

6. Antihistamine spray
Occasionally, a ferret will be stung by a bee, wasp or other such insect which has managed to find its way into the ferret's cage. The sting should be removed and antihistamine applied.

7. Cotton wool
Used for cleaning wounds, cuts and abrasions and for stemming the flow of blood.

8. Surgical gauze
Used for padding wounds and stemming the flow of blood.

9. Adhesive plasters
Although these will soon be chewed off by the ferret, they are useful for applying directly to small wounds and for keeping dressings in place. They can also be used for minor splinting.

10. Bandages
A selection of small bandages should be kept for binding broken limbs and wounds. They will, of course, be temporary as the ferret will chew them off.

11. Cotton buds
Ideal for cleaning wounds and the application of ointments etc. With care, they can also be used to clean the pinnae (ear flaps) but *under no circumstances* should you poke these (or any other object) down the ear canal.

12. Table salt
A solution of table salt (two teaspoons of salt to 0.5 litres of water) is a good solution to wash debris from wounds and to counter infection.

13. Sodium bicarbonate
On a wet compress, this will help reduce swelling.

14. Alcohol (surgical spirit)
Useful for the removal of ticks etc.

15. Styptic pencil
To help stem the flow of blood.

Many of the items listed can be used on either ferret *OR* human injuries.

Common Diseases and Ailments

The following is a list, in alphabetical order, of some of the most common diseases and ailments which may afflict ferrets. It is not intended to be a 'do-it-yourself guide to medicine', merely to help owners recognise any potentially dangerous symptoms in their ferrets. I have also included information on preventative measures which should be taken to avoid medical problems. In all cases of ill or injured ferrets, I strongly recommend that you seek the advice of a qualified veterinary surgeon; do not delay this, as such time lapses can often lead to a sick ferret going beyond the point where a vet can save the animal. Time waited is time wasted.

Aleutian disease
This disease is caused by a parvovirus and is an immune deficiency disease. It takes its name from the Aleutian strain of mink in which it was first discovered in the USA in 1956, although it is believed that there is now a specific ferret strain of this disease. Since 1956, cases have been recorded in Canada and New Zealand. The first cases reported in the UK were in early 1990, probably via mink imported from the USA. No true connection has ever been proven between these imported mink and AD in ferrets, but vets and MAFF officials still retain their suspicions that this is the case.

Aleutian disease is described as being transmitted both vertically and horizontally, ie it can pass from parents to off-spring and also from unrelated ferrets to other ferrets; this latter type of transmission occurs through body fluids. These can be saliva, blood, urine, faeces and aerosol droplets from the lungs, via sneezing, coughing and even simply breathing. This aerosol transmission can occur up to a metre away from the infected animal. It is obvious that hobs (males) should not be shared in breeding programmes, as this is an almost guaranteed method of transmitting the disease; neither should hoblets (vasectomized males) be shared between kennels of ferrets. (Hoblets are used to bring the jill out of oestrus, without getting her pregnant — a vital operation if the jill is not to succumb to many of the ailments that prolonged oestrus can cause in ferrets ; see 'Oestrogen induced anaemia'). The numbers of animals reported as infected with AD are tiny.

Symptoms vary tremendously and may include black tarry faeces, weight loss, aggressiveness, recurrent fevers, thyroiditis, posterior paralysis, and eventual death; in stressed animals, death may occur suddenly. There is no specific treatment, but antibiotics and steroids may give temporary relief. Diagnosis of this disease in a living ferret can be confirmed by serology, the necessary blood being obtained by clipping the toe nails in such a manner that, using a capillary tube, a vet can obtain blood from the animal. With dead animals, a post-mortem examination, which should always be conducted in the case of a sudden or unexplained death, or where a disease is suspected of causing the death, will be necessary to confirm the diagnosis. No ferret having suffered Aleutian disease should be bred from.

Alopecia (hair loss)

This is often caused by the feeding of too many raw eggs, which contain a compound which inhibits biotin, resulting in this condition. There are also many other causes of hair loss in ferrets, including seasonal environmental changes, and it is recommended that any ferrets manifesting such symptoms be given a thorough examination by a qualified vet. (See also 'Mites'.)

Hair loss on the tail can occur in either sex and at any age, ranging from a very small area of the tail to the compete tail, and in most case, the naked skin is seen to have black spots on it; these are blocked pores — 'blackheads'. Usually, though not always, such hair loss occurs when the animal is in its moult of late summer or early autumn and may last for up to three to four months; the condition is also often to be seen when the spring moult occurs. Not all ferrets in the same cage will be affected, and even affected ferrets are not necessarily affected every year.

Veterinary tests in many affected animals have not shown any reason or causal agents, and it is believed that the condition is simply a case of excessive moult. If in doubt, consult your vet.

Abscesses

Abscesses are simply wounds which have filled with pus, the bacteria *Staphylococcus* and *Streptococcus* being the usual cause. They can be caused by a variety of occurrences, such as bites, cuts or damage to the inside of the mouth caused by bones in the ferret's diet. In order to prevent wounds developing into abscesses, ensure that they are thoroughly cleaned and disinfected. Once abscesses have developed, they will require lancing and draining, often several times, and it may be necessary for the animal to be given a course of broad-spectrum antibiotics, such as ampicillin. Obviously, action of this type must only be taken by a qualified veterinary surgeon.

Actinomycosis

An acute hard swelling of the ferret's neck, actinomycosis is probably caused by abrasions to the animal's oesophagus, usually by feeding too many day-old chicks in the diet. Affected ferrets will be listless, anorexic and have a fever (a temperature of up to 40.8°C is not uncommon). Refer the animal to a vet who will probably administer injections of cephalosporin; you will then have to keep the ferret nourished on a liquid diet until full recovery is achieved.

Bites and stings

These need to be split into four categories — insect, snake, rat or ferret.

Insect bites (including stings)

Clip a little fur away from the area so that you can actually see the problem, then wash with saline solution. Bees leave their sting in the victim, wasps do not. If there is a sting present, it should be carefully removed with the tweezers and then the area wiped with cotton wool (or a cotton bud) soaked in alcohol, such as surgical spirit. For wasp stings, a little vinegar will prove beneficial, while for bee stings use a little bicarbonate of soda. Dry the area thoroughly, and use an antihistamine spray or apply a wet compress to help reduce the irritation and swelling.

If the ferret has been bitten or stung in the throat, veterinary attention must be sought as soon as possible; such stings can cause swelling that may block the airways and thus kill the ferret.

Rat bites

Rat bites are one of the most dangerous of all bites that a working ferret may suffer. Rats can carry many harmful diseases and so it is essential that no risks are taken.

Clip away the fur from around the wound, ensuring that the clippings do not become entangled in the wound itself. Wetting the scissors is recommended, as the hairs stick to the blades rather than falling onto the wound; dipping the scissors into a jug of water after each snip will remove all hairs from the metal. Thoroughly clean the area of the wound with a saline solution and then an antiseptic liquid; dry and apply liberal amounts of antibiotic dusting powder. If the wound is large, or you have good reason to believe that the rat was infected, take the injured ferret to the vet as soon as possible after the injury where the vet may well administer an injection of antibiotics. I would always recommend this action after any rat bite — better safe than sorry!

Snake bites

There are many venomous snakes and, although it is unusual for ferrets or dogs to be bitten by these reptiles, it does sometimes happen. During the spring or early summer the snakes are rather lethargic, especially the gravid (pregnant) females. At such time, they will keep still as long as possible, even when approached. If your ferret or dog does not see the snake and stands on it, the snake will bite. It is most important that you keep the injured animal as calm as possible (and you must also remain calm as your actions will influence the animal), and seek immediate medical attention.

Ferret bites

Although it may at first seem strange, ferrets are more likely to suffer from bites from other ferrets than from any other animal, especially so during the breeding season, when the hob takes hold of the jill by the scruff, hanging on tightly and, very often, breaking the jill's skin with his teeth. These types of injuries are not usually serious, providing that they are given first-aid treatment as soon as possible.

The area of the bite must be clipped of fur, and the wound thoroughly washed with a saline solution followed by an antiseptic liquid. A good dusting with an antibiotic wound powder will finish the job. If action is not taken, the wound may fester and result in abscesses.

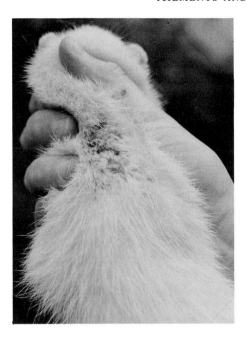

The most common injury to ferrets is a bite on the back of the neck, inflicted (usually during mating) by another ferret.

Bleeding
NEVER apply tourniquets. (See Cuts)

Botulism
Botulism is a killer. The disease is caused by one of the most common bacterium known to science, *Clostridium botulinum*, usually 'Type C', a natural contaminant of most wild bird cadavers. When this bacterium comes into contact with any decaying flesh (ie meat), it causes a deadly toxin to be formed. If this flesh is then eaten by an animal, the toxin affects its victim by attacking the animal's nervous system causing paralysis, at first usually in the hind legs. Eventually, this paralysis will affect the body's vital organs, and leads inevitably to the death of the affected animal. There is no cure or treatment for this, and ferrets are among the most susceptible animals to botulism.

In order to try to prevent this deadly disease, pay particular attention to the meat that you feed; defrost frozen meat and feed immediately. If there is any doubt whatsoever about the meat, boil it for at least fifteen minutes before feeding. Botulism is not contagious and sometimes only one animal of a group may succumb to the illness. If for whatever reason you believe that your ferrets have a high risk of this disease, it is possible to have an annual toxoid injection to provide some protection for your ferrets.

Breathing problems
Ferrets gasping for breath are obviously showing symptoms of some form of breathing difficulty; this may be heatstroke (see 'the sweats'), fluid on the lungs or an obstruction of some kind. Many obstructions can be removed from a ferret's mouth with a cotton bud or even a finger.

Artificial respiration, though difficult, is possible with ferrets. If a ferret has stopped breathing, rather than give mouth-to-mouth respiration, hold the ferret by its hind legs and, keeping your arms straight, swing the animal to left and then to right. This transfers the weight of the ferret's internal organs on and off the diaphragm, causing the lungs to fill and empty of air. Keep this up until the ferret begins breathing on its own, help arrives, or you believe the ferret to be beyond help.

Convulsions
Convulsions are a symptom, an indication that the ferret has an infection of some kind or has been poisoned, and *not* a disease. There are obviously many possible causes for convulsions, and one of the most common in captive ferrets is heatstroke, or the 'sweats'. However, if your ferret is suffering from convulsions, you should seek urgent medical attention for the ailing animal.

Cuts, abrasions and other wounds
There are several different types of wound which a ferret may suffer, and each requires a slightly different technique.

Incised (clean) cut
These are straight cuts, as one would get from a sharp knife blade; as such, they bleed profusely. This bleeding, which can be very frightening to people not used to such things — a little blood appears as 'gallons' to most lay people, even though there may only be a thimble full! — helps clean the wound of debris, and this lessens the possibility of infection.

Bleeding should be stemmed by direct pressure, if at all possible; where it is not, apply indirect pressure on an artery at the heart side of the wound. Elevating the injury will enable gravity to help reduce the blood flow. Apply a suitable dressing; large and/or deep cuts will almost certainly require sutures (stitches) from a qualified vet.

Lacerated cuts
These are tears in the skin, as caused by barbed wire, for instance, and will bleed less profusely than incised cuts. The big danger is that the injury will have pushed dirt and debris into the wound, and the lack of bleeding will mean that the dirt is not washed out. You must clean the wound with a saline solution (salt water — 2 teaspoonfuls to 0.5 litres of warm water); dry it and apply dressing if necessary.

Contusion (bruise)
This is a sign of internal bleeding, and a careful watch must be kept on the injured animal. If shock sets in, seek veterinary advice immediately.

Puncture (stab)
Puncture wounds, which can be caused by nails, slivers of wood and other such objects, usually appear very small at the surface but, of course, could be very deep. *Never* remove any object from a wound, as this may aggravate the injury and/or allow

large amounts of bleeding. Apply pressure around the wound site, using a dressing to maintain the pressure, and seek medical attention immediately.

Gunshot wounds
If you work your ferret, then it is quite possible that they may be accidentally shot. The most common type of wound to a working ferret is from a shotgun, in which case the animal will be peppered with balls of shot, which will all require removal; bleeding should not be profuse. The other type of wound is from a solid projectile, ie a bullet. Bullets make two wounds — one in and one out. Where 'sporting' (hollow point) ammunition is used, the exit wound will be several times larger than the entry wound.

In all cases of gunshot wound, stem the flow of blood, keep the animal calm, checking for signs of trauma, and seek veterinary treatment immediately.

Dental problems
Ferrets, like humans, have teeth, and also, like humans, occasionally have dental problems. They occasionally damage their teeth, either while working or even in their cage when chewing the wire mesh; gingivitis, a gum disorder, is also quite common in ferrets. The build-up of food debris often leads to dental problems, and the diet of the ferret is, therefore, an important factor in the condition of the teeth. Any problems with a ferret's teeth must be treated by a properly qualified vet.

Diarrhoea
Diarrhoea is a symptom and *not* a disease; it is indicative of a problem, which may be serious or minor, but will still require investigation. In ferrets this condition is often referred to as the 'scours', and is usually, but of course not always, a sign that the animal has been fed on a poor diet, or its food is contaminated. Feeding milk sops, too many raw eggs, too much fat, a sudden and abrupt change of diet and food which has gone off all have the effect of scouring a ferret. Diarrhoea can also be indicative of some other, more serious affliction, such as poisoning, internal parasites or even stress.

If you are feeding your ferrets a proper balanced diet of fresh, or freshly defrosted, cadavers, they should not suffer from loose motions as a matter of course. If you have been feeding them on a diet of bread and milk, their motions will almost always be soft (often liquid), light brown in colour, and extremely smelly. If fed on the diet which I have recommended in the chapter on feeding, their motions will be solid, almost black, and have little smell. Keep a record of everything you feed them, particularly anything out of the ordinary.

Diarrhoea causes the animal to dehydrate, and can lead to irreparable body damage (particularly of the kidneys), and even death. You should isolate the affected ferret(s) and keep them on a water and electrolyte (a solution of essential minerals) regime for twenty-four hours, dosing with kaolin solution about every two hours. After the fast, food intake should be gradually built up again; do *not* put the animals straight back on their original diet, otherwise the whole problem may recur. Chicken, rabbit and fish are excellent 'invalid' foods, and ideal for this task.

If the diarrhoea persists, or if there is blood in the motions, the vet must be consulted immediately.

Distemper, canine (CD) (Hard Pad)

Ferrets are highly susceptible to canine distemper, a virus which is one of the most common fatal diseases in ferrets; dogs are the most common source of such an infection, with the incubation period being between seven to nine days. In some countries, owners have their animals vaccinated against this disease as a matter of course, while in others this does not happen. Indeed, in some countries there is no distemper vaccine licensed for use in ferrets; the use of an unsuitable vaccine may have fatal results. If you are considering this preventative course of action, consult your vet.

Symptoms of the disease are swollen feet, leading to hard pad, the actual thickening of the soles of the feet and a classical sign of distemper infection; runny eyes and nose, diarrhoea, lack of appetite, a larger than average thirst and a rash, usually under the chin. In its latter stages, the infected animal will vomit, have convulsions and, shortly before dying, will pass into a coma.

This disease is highly contagious and, at the first signs of distemper, all infected ferrets must be isolated. Ensure that you thoroughly disinfect your hands after handling a sick animal; as the name suggests, dogs can also contract this disease, and it is all too easy to spread it. Immediate veterinary advice must be sought, although only very mild cases can be treated; it is often kinder, both to the infected ferrets and the others in your care, to have the infected ferret put down once the diagnosis is confirmed by a vet.

Enteritis

Enteritis is an inflammation of the intestines, causing diarrhoea, and is very common among kits and young stock. If your ferrets are experiencing diarrhoea, and show signs of blood in their faeces, this may indicate this condition. It can be caused by different things but, usually, it is the bacterium *Escherichia coli,* often referred to by its abbreviated name of *E.coli*, and formerly known to science as *Bacillus coli*. Immediate treatment with a broad spectrum antibiotic, supplemented with regular doses of kaolin, may cure this condition. If left untreated, the affected animal will most definitely die.

Another major cause of enteritis is *Campylobacter*; in humans, this type of 'food poisoning' is known as dysentery. The most effective antibiotics for use against this are chloramphenicol and gentamicin.

As mentioned under the heading of 'diarrhoea', affected animals must be given large amounts of water and electrolyte to avoid the dangers of dehydration.

Foot-rot

This condition was extremely common until a few years ago, and in some areas is still a major problem. It is usually caused solely by keeping ferrets in dirty, wet conditions, allowing a mite, *Sarcoptes scabiei*, to infect the animals. The symptoms of foot-rot are swollen, scabby feet and, if left untreated, the claws will eventually drop off. Affected animals must be isolated immediately, and all other ferrets — especially those kept in the same cage — examined. All bedding and wood shavings must be removed from the cage and burned, with the cage itself being thoroughly disinfected with a suitable disinfectant.

Veterinary treatment must be sought for all infected ferrets, as home treatment is only very rarely effective; time waited is time wasted.

Fractures

Fractures are caused by either direct or indirect pressure on the bones, which may crack or actually break. Where the bone is broken and pierces the skin, this is known as an open or compound fracture, and all others as closed fractures. Signs of such injury are obvious — painful movement of the limb, tenderness, swelling, loss of control of the limb, deformity of the limb, unnatural movement of the limb, and crepitus (the sensation or, in very bad cases, the sound of the two ends of the bones grinding on each other).

Keep the patient quiet and steady and support the injured limb, immobilising it with bandages and splints if necessary, to prevent it moving and causing greater damage. Raising the limb will help reduce discomfort and swelling (by reducing the blood flow).

Hard pad see 'Distemper'

Heatstroke (the 'sweats')

Ferrets cannot tolerate high temperatures, reacting adversely to too much heat, and may well die from heatstroke, often referred to as 'the sweats', a rather misleading term since ferrets cannot sweat. As in all things, prevention is better than cure, and the siting of the cage (as discussed in an earlier chapter) is very important, as is the position that they are left in while out working. In the confines of a carrying-box or even a motor car, the temperature can quickly rise to a dangerous level, even in the cooler sunshine of autumn and spring. No animals should be left unattended in a vehicle, or transported in such a manner that they or their carrying-box is in full sunlight. Remember, the sun does not stay in the same position throughout the day, and that, even if the box or car is in the shadows when you leave it, it may not stay that way for long. When you return, your ferrets may well be dead.

In extreme summer temperatures, or in areas where it is known that temperatures will be high, every effort must be made to insulate the cage, and place it in an area where it and its inmates are protected from the full effect of varying temperatures. Where it is not possible to keep the ferrets' cage as cool as one would like, wet cloths may be hung over the cage to keep the temperature down, although they will soon dry out, and so require constant attention throughout the day. Placing bricks on each corner of the cage roof, and then positioning a piece of timber over them, will act as 'double-glazing', and will be extremely effective in reducing heat build-up in the cage.

The first sign of heatstroke or heat exhaustion is an agitated ferret in obvious distress. If in their cage, affected ferrets will stretch out and pant heavily; if left untreated, they will eventually collapse, pass into a coma and die.

Immediately a ferret shows symptoms of heatstroke, you must act — and fast; delay can be fatal. The ferret's body is over heating, and so your first task must be to lower its body temperature. With mildly affected ferrets, simply moving them to a cool area and ensuring a steady passage of cool air over them, is usually effective; a light spraying with cold water from a plant mister is beneficial. In bad cases, where it is literally make or break, I find that the best method is to immerse the animal to the neck in a bucket of cold water, repeating this procedure regularly for the next few minutes, by which time the ferret should be showing signs of recovery. Ensure that the ferret is thoroughly dried, and placed in a cage in a cool area, with a small amount of hay for bedding; this hay will also help to dry the ferret's coat. This is a very drastic 'treatment', and should only be attempted where the animal is very badly affected.

In all cases, it is vital to keep the head cool, as brain death can occur — the brain is quite literally 'cooked'. Veterinary advice should be sought at the earliest opportunity.

Hypocalcaemia

This is caused by a lack of calcium in the blood. It can occur three to four weeks after the jill has given birth. Posterior paralysis and convulsions are common symptoms, while the cause is usually due to poor diet; feeding a diet heavily dependent on day-old chicks will almost certainly lead to this complaint. Consult your veterinary surgeon immediately; they will probably administer an intraperitoneal injection of calcium borogluconate, which gives a speedy response in affected animals. After this injection, a calcium-rich diet is essential for total recovery.

Influenza

Ferrets are susceptible to human influenza, and can catch influenza ('the 'flu') from their owners, or vice versa.

Symptoms in ferrets are the same as in humans — fever, sneezing, lack of appetite, listlessness, runny eyes and a nasal discharge. In adult ferrets the condition is not usually serious with most ferrets making a spontaneous recovery, although antibiotics may be necessary to control some secondary infections. Influenza is, however, almost always fatal in young ferrets.

Infected ferrets must be isolated to prevent spread of this condition. The wearing of a mask by humans will help prevent the crossing of the infection from ferret to human, and vice versa.

Leptospirosis

The ferret has a natural resistance to this disease, often called 'rat catcher's yellows' or 'Weil's disease', and is highly unlikely to contract it. Consequently, vaccinations for leptospirosis are unnecessary and should not be used.

Leukaemia

This disease is often found in unmated jills, but is almost completely undetectable until the ferret is almost at death's door. The presence of any 'lumps' in the animal's groin or abdomen, or under the jaw may indicate this disease. Medical advice should be sought immediately. See also 'oestrogen-induced anaemia'.

Mange See 'Mites'.

Mastitis
This is the inflammation of the jill's mammary glands, and often occurs when the jill is in the early stages of feeding young. It is a very painful condition that requires immediate medical attention. The glands become very swollen and hard and the kits can obtain very little, if any, milk. Unless it is cleared up quickly, the kits will probably die and the jill will, at best, be very ill. The disease is caused by infection by *E. coli* and treatment usually consists of antibiotics, preferably ampicillin.

Mites
Mites have unpleasant effects on the ferret and there are three types commonly found on the animal.

Sarcoptes scabiei causes two types of mange in ferrets, which can become infected through coming into direct contact with other infected animals, such as rodents, or simply by being on infected ground. One type of mange (sarcoptic) causes alopecia and pruritus (an intense itching), while the other causes only foot or toe problems ('foot-rot'). The first sign of mange is persistent scratching, even though there is no obvious cause such as fleas. Eventually, the skin will become very red and sore, a symptom that is easier to notice in albino ferrets than in ones with polecat coloration. As the disease progresses, these sores cause baldness and the sores become even worse.

A parasiticidal wash (eg bromocyclen) must be applied to the affected areas, or injections of ivermectin administered; this drug cannot be used in the first month of pregnancy, or it will cause congenital defects. The cage must be thoroughly treated, soaking it in a strong solution of disinfectant or bleach, which must be washed off before any ferret is returned to the cage.

Be warned — mange can be contracted by humans, when it is known as scabies.

Ear mites, *Otodectes cynotis*, are common in ferrets and can easily be treated with ear drops which contain gamma BHC or with ivermectin injections. If your ferrets seem to spend a lot of time scratching their ears, an investigation is called for. A build-up of wax in the ears, dotted with black specks, is a sure indication that ferrets have ear mites; the black specks are probably spots of dried blood, and the ear mites are usually white or colourless and are not visible to the naked eye — a magnifying lens or otoscope being required. If left untreated, the irritation caused by these mites will cause the ferret to scratch, sometimes until its ears actually bleed. The mites can move down the aural canal and infect the middle ear; such an infection will cause the affected animal to lose its sense of balance. This may be indicated either by the ferret simply being unable to hold its head straight or, in more serious cases, by constantly falling over.

It is important that all ferrets that have been in contact with the infected ferret are also treated, as ear mites can infect other animals who may not show any symptoms for some time.

Seek veterinary advice in all cases of ear mite, loss of balance etc.

The harvest mite, *Trombicula autumnalis*, can cause sores on the underside of the neck and trunk of ferrets, particularly during the autumn period; a wash in a bromocyclen-based product will be effective.

Oestrogen-induced anaemia

When a jill is not mated the levels of oestrogen, the female sex hormone, in her body will rise and can have serious effects on the health of the ferret, often causing progressive depression of the bone marrow and sometimes resulting in a condition known as pancytopoenia — the abnormal depression of all three elements of blood — which is debilitating and potentially fatal. Signs include weight loss, alopecia, anorexia, pale lips and gums, difficulty in breathing and, in later stages, darkening of faeces (caused by blood), and bleeding sores on the animal's flanks and abdomen. There may also be secondary infections.

In its advanced stages, treatment is highly unlikely to be effective, but in early stages, spaying or hormonal treatment to stop oestrus may be used, and repeated transfusions of fresh whole blood containing 1 ml of sodium citrate can be used effectively.

Again, prevention is better than cure, and jills which it is not wished to breed from should be neutered (spayed), or given drugs (eg proligestone), or served with a hoblet (a vasectomised male ferret). The latter will almost certainly result in a 'phantom pregnancy' (pseudo-pregnancy) which will last for the full forty-two day term, after which the jill will return to oestrus, and need to be served again.

Osteodystrophy

Defective bone formations, often due to hyperphosphorosis (too much phosphorous in the diet) is caused by feeding a diet consisting entirely of, or rich in, muscle meat; this lacks calcium, and leads to a deficiency of this vital mineral. The problem usually manifests itself in young ferrets (six to twelve weeks) who have difficulty walking, moving instead with the gait of a seal, with the legs (particularly the front legs) sticking out to the side of the body rather than pointing to the floor; death is common. As the bones of such animals are soft and deformed, the ferrets never completely recover, and will always have deformed legs and spine, making movement awkward, difficult and painful. A top quality vitamin and mineral supplement can help, but it is better to prevent the problem by feeding a diet of complete cadavers rather than 'meat'. Veterinary advice must, of course, be sought whenever ferrets have difficulty walking in a normal manner.

Parasites

Even the most pampered ferrets can suffer from the unwanted attentions of parasites, either internal (endoparasites) or external (ectoparasites). Ferrets can suffer from worms, *Toxocara* or *Toxascaris*, but these are not usually problematical. A vet will prescribe an anthelmintic (an agent which is destructive to worms) such as mebenda-zole or fenbenzadole.

Heart worms, coccidia, *Toxiplasma*, and *Pneumocystis* are sometimes found. Veterinary examination, and clinical investigation of the faeces will be necessary to positively identify the actual problem.

The first signs of a worm infestation are an insatiable appetite coupled with a steady loss of weight. Sometimes, segments of the worms may be found in the ferret's faeces before other symptoms indicate a problem. Do *not* attempt to treat ferrets with powders and doses that your local pet shop may recommend for a dog. Seek veteri-nary advice.

Fleas — *Ctenocephalides*, and ticks — *Ixodes ricinus*, are external parasites that most working ferrets will catch at some stage, especially if used for hunting. These ectopar-asites are contracted from other animals such as dogs, cats, rabbits and other such species. Insecticidal preparations intended for dogs and cats are safe to use on ferrets. With new preparations coming on to the market all the time, care must always be taken to ensure that any product is safe *before* you use it on your ferrets. Do not forget that you will have to adjust the dosage to suit the size of the ferret, as per the manu-facturer's instructions.

A flea, an unwelcome visitor which every ferret will host at some time in their life.

All of the bedding and wood shavings from the ferret's cage must be removed and burned and the cage thoroughly disinfected. Use the powder as a prophylactic (pre-ventative measure) to treat all shavings, bedding and even the cage itself. Do *not* use such powders and sprays in any cage where a jill is still feeding her kits, as there is a danger of poisoning the litter.

Ticks are rather more difficult to deal with than fleas, but they do respond to some sprays and powders, although in some countries these may only be available from veterinary surgeons. Care must be taken to ensure that the mouth parts of ticks are completely removed from the ferret's skin, otherwise infection and abscesses can occur; never simply pull ticks out. Paint alcohol on the tick using a fine paint brush, and the tick should have died and dropped off within twenty-four hours; if not, simply repeat the process.

Although some authorities suggest that ticks be burned off with a lighted cigarette, this should never be attempted. It is all too easy to burn the ferret with the cigarette and the alcohol method is much more effective, with none of the dangers.

There are now a number of devices on the market which have been specifically designed to remove ticks, due mainly to concern regarding Lyme's disease in humans. These are a type of sprung forceps which grip the tick around the head; the device is then gently twisted backwards and forwards, until the tick comes out. I have tested several such implements and have had complete success with each; I now keep one in my first-aid kit.

Posterior paralysis ('the staggers')

The causes of paralysis in ferrets are many and varied, including disease of the spinal disks, hypocalcaemia (lack of calcium in the blood), Aleutian disease, viral myelitis (inflammation of the spinal cord), cancer of the spine, vertebral trauma, or even a dietary deficiency. It is often caused by injury and paralysis can also be inherited. If the latter is the case, the disorder will show itself in young litters. There is usually no cure for this and it is, therefore, best to have the animals destroyed. The parents of such litters should not be used for breeding again.

In all cases of paralysis, veterinary advice must be sought immediately.

Pregnancy toxaemia

Leading to the sudden death of the jill just before she is due to give birth, the cause of this problem is currently unknown but is probably linked to a poor diet.

Pyometra

This is the accumulation of pus within the uterus and is only occasionally seen in ferrets; when it does occur, it is immediately after the start of a pseudo-pregnancy. Organisms responsible for this condition in ferrets include *Streptococcus*, *Staphylococcus*, *E. coli Corynebacterium*.

Affected ferrets will be anorexic, lethargic, and will often have a fever. Medical attention must be sought immediately, as the uterus may rupture, causing peritonitis and an ovariohysterectomy will be required urgently.

Rabies

In countries where this disease is prevalent, ferrets can become infected. Clinical signs of the disease include lethargy, posterior paralysis and anxiety; recovery of infected ferrets is not unusual.

A ferret with a tick on its head.

The removal of the tick with a purpose-made tool. It is vital that all such parasites are removed completely as soon as they are discovered.

117

Ringworm (dermatophytosis)

Although rare, this condition is occasionally seen in ferrets. It is always contracted by contact with an infected cat or, extremely rarely, dog. Caused by the fungus *Microsporum canis*, this disease is not caused by a worm, as many are led to believe by its name. The condition manifests itself with hair loss and bald, scaly patches of skin. This disease is a fungal infection. Home treatment is sometimes successful, but it is strongly recommended that veterinary advice is sought. As the condition is transmissible to man, it must be treated immediately.

(See also 'Mites').

Sarcoptic mange See 'Mites'.

Scours See 'Diarrhoea'

Shock

Shock, which is an acute fall in blood pressure, is often evident after the ferret has been involved in an accident or has been injured; certain diseases can also cause this condition. It manifests itself with cool skin, pale lips and gums (due to the lack of circulation); faint, rapid pulse; staring but unseeing eyes.

The victim must be kept warm and the blood circulation returned to normal as soon as possible. Massaging the ferret will help circulation, and wrapping it in a towel or blanket will help keep it warm. The affected animal should be kept quiet and warm, and veterinary treatment sought as soon as possible.

Skin tumours (neoplasia)

Common in ferrets, in all cases surgery is necessary and should be carried out as soon as possible. These tumours are, however, very difficult to eliminate and frequently recur. Warts also occur on ferrets and so it is vital that histopathology is used to confirm all diagnoses. Consult your vet if any animal develops lumps anywhere on its body.

'The staggers' See 'Posterior paralysis'

Thiamine deficiency

Where ferrets are fed a diet consisting of a large proportion of day-old chicks, raw fish or eggs (or a combination of any or all of these items), a thiamine deficiency is almost guaranteed. Symptoms include anorexia, lethargy, weakness of the hindquarters, and convulsions. Injections of the vitamin B complex usually have a rapid effect, and recovery is usually total. Avoid this problem by supplying your ferrets with a proper diet. All cases of convulsions, paralysis or unusual behaviour should be referred to your vet.

Tuberculosis

Ferrets are susceptible to avian, bovine and human tuberculosis, with symptoms which include paralysis of the limbs, diarrhoea and wasting of the body. Almost always fatal, the disease is highly contagious; contact your vet at once if you suspect this condition in your ferrets.

Urolithiasis (gall stones)

Varying in size from a particle of sand to quite a large stone, gall stones sometimes occur in ferrets. Treatment consists of antibiotics, surgery and the use of special diets to dissolve the stone.

Zinc toxicity

Ferrets cannot tolerate high levels of zinc and may become ill through the use of galvanised feeding dishes or even by licking cage bars. Symptoms include anaemia, lethargy and weakness of the hind legs; liver and kidney failure can quickly follow and so all suspected cases should be referred to a vet as soon as possible, although there is no actual treatment and affected animals are unlikely to recover. It is common for vets to advise euthanasia for affected ferrets to avoid undue suffering.

****

In many cases health problems are avoidable, and the best way to ensure healthy ferrets is to indulge in good husbandry, including the provision of an adequate balanced diet. Ferrets have the disturbing habit of often not showing any symptoms until they are almost dead. If you suspect any of your stock of 'sickening', contact your veterinary surgeon without delay; time waited is time wasted.

Chapter 10

Genetics

Many people fight shy of genetics, thinking that the subject must be incredibly difficult and that to understand it, one will require a degree in zoology; this is simply not
true. Once certain basic rules and principles have been learned, a few technical terms
committed to memory, and a little common sense applied, the subject will be seen to
be extremely logical and quite easy. Too many people, both in the ferret fancy and
other fancies, will not make this effort, preferring to fumble along, perhaps asking
'experts' for advice from time to time. However, if you do not have a good (ie
working) knowledge of genetics, your breeding programme will never be more than
moderately successful in the long term. At best, you will produce ferrets of average
quality, at worst you will produce ferrets that cannot be passed on, and yet are useless
to yourself.

Basics

Within the scope of this book, I will only attempt to guide the reader through the
basics of the subject. However, once you have grasped those basics, life will be easier
and, if you wish, you will be in a position to take your studies further.

It is necessary firstly to understand that *every* animal receives a half of its inherited
traits from each parent. Sometimes, for reasons that we shall discuss later, it may
seem that some offspring inherit more qualities and characteristics from one parent
than from the other, but this is not so.

The inherited components are known as genes, which are carried on the chromosomes, rather like beads on a string. It is the job of the genes to tell the cells of the
body how to behave — to change shape, to grow or to change colour, for instance.
In the ferret, there are forty (ie twenty pairs) of chromosomes. Along this string of
beads are points known as 'locii' and, normally, each locus is occupied by the same
gene.

Sex Chromosomes

One pair of chromosomes determine the sex of the individual, and are logically
known as the sex chromosomes (all the others are known as autosomes). The male
chromosome is referred to as Y, while the female chromosome is known as X. A
female ferret will have two X chromosomes (XX), and the male will have one X and
one Y chromosome (XY). Obviously then, it is the male's chromosomes which influence the sex of any progeny, and the resultant ferret has a fifty-fifty chance of being
male, and exactly the same chance of being female.

At fertilisation, the germ cells (the female egg and the male sperm) contain twenty
single chromosomes each (due to a process called meiosis) so that, on fertilisation, the

resultant zygote contains 20 PAIRS again, as will every cell (except the germ cells) of every individual ferret.

Once fertilised, the egg (now known as a zygote) grows and develops into a young ferret. This growth is accomplished by progressive division of the cell, the number of cells doubling at every stage ie 2, 4, 8, 16, 32 etc, until the resultant tissue takes on the appearance of an identifiable foetus. When the cells divide, the chromosomes are 'shuffled', so that the genes which accompany them can form new, as well as established, combinations. It is not known exactly how many genes are carried on a chromosome, but some authorities believe that it could be tens of thousands. Such large numbers are necessary to control all of the physiological functions of the body, as each can only act in a very simple manner, and so vast quantities of them are required to control bodily functions.

Mutations

Obviously, the constant creation of new cells means that the chromosomes (and hence the genes) are being constantly duplicated. These duplications usually go according to plan, and the copy made is an exact copy. However, very rarely (about once in a million copies), a slight copying error may occur. This means that a duplicated gene is slightly different from its predecessor. Remember that genes control the functions and appearance of an individual, and so a changed gene could result in a noticeable difference in the animal concerned, eg coat colour, type of fur etc.

Such an abrupt change, where it results in a change in appearance of the individual, is referred to as a 'sport', 'mutation', or 'mutant'. As far as we, as ferret breeders are concerned, the mutations that would most interest us are those which result in either a change in appearance, or have a detrimental effect on the ferrets. When a mutation occurs, thus creating a 'mutant allele', this mutant allele will occupy the same locus as its normal cousin did. During cell division (ie growth), some genes may 'crossover' from one chromosome to the other chromosome. Obviously, genes which are close together on the chromosome will be less likely to crossover than those that are far apart. Two genes on the same chromosome are said to show 'linkage', and the degree of linkage is an indication of the distance between the genes, ie the closer together, the stronger the linkage.

Mendelian Genetics

Gregor Mendel was a member of the Augustinian monastery in Brünn, in Austria (now known as Brno, in the Czech Republic). In 1856, he carried out a vast number of experiments on hereditary factors, choosing the garden pea (*Pisum sativum*) as his subject. This plant has a number of easily identifiable characteristics — wrinkled and smooth seeds; long and short stems; red and white flowers etc — and he carefully cross pollinated these and meticulously recorded the results over many years. From these results Mendel drew several conclusions, and these form the foundations for today's understanding of heredity. He described his work in an obscure natural history journal in 1866. It wasn't until 1900, however, that the scientific world became aware of Mendel's findings, but today 'Mendelian

Genetics' form the foundation of all of the work that has been, and still is being, carried out on heredity.

All chromosomes, and therefore all genes, are present twice in the individual, but only once in the germ cells. At its simplest, genetics concerns the passing on from one generation to the next of several characteristics. In order to grasp the principles involved, we must take the subject one step at a time. We will, therefore, look at the way in which a single characteristic is passed on. This is known as 'monohybrid inheritance'.

Monohybrid Inheritance

Let us take an example of a pair of *pure* (ie true-bred) polecat-coloured ferrets mating together. As all of the inherited material passed on to the next generation must be the same (as regards colour and markings, ie polecat), then all of the young must also inherit these characteristics. When these ferrets breed with each other, again they can only inherit the same colour and markings — polecat.

Four polecat kits, born to a captured polecat jill three weeks after capture and belonging to the author. A true-bred line will be kept, while the males will also be hybridised with some of the author's ferret jills.

Suppose, however, that we mated a pure polecat-coloured ferret with a pure albino. It is obvious that, given that the progeny from any mating will always inherit fifty per cent of its traits from each parent, the litter will all be carrying genes for both polecat *and* albino (the first litter in a series of litters bred for genetic purposes is always referred to as F1; the second as F2; the third as F3 etc, the 'F' standing for 'filial'). However, some genes dominate others; these are known as dominant genes, while those which are dominated, are known as recessive. Recessive genes will only show themselves when the animal has two helpings of that recessive gene, ie is pure-bred. This can only happen when *both* parents possess this gene. The polecat gene, as it is the original (natural or normal) colour is always dominant to all other colours. Therefore, when the two come together, although the genetic make-up (the genotype) of the ferrets is both polecat and albino, the physical appearance (the phenotype) is that of a polecat, as this gene effectively masks the action of the albino gene.

As in most jobs, practitioners use their own form of shorthand, and the geneticist is certainly no exception. All *mutant* genes are given a letter; dominant genes are signified by using an upper case (capital) letter, while recessive genes are given a lower case letter. If an animal carrying a mutant gene is mated to an animal *not* carrying that gene, then the shorthand used to designate the ferret not carrying the mutant gene would be the reverse of that for the ferret that *is* carrying that gene, ie the shorthand for the gene that produces the albino is 'aa'; if such an animal were to be mated with a pure-bred polecat-coloured ferret, that is obviously *not* carrying that recessive gene, the genotype of the polecat-coloured ferret would be given as 'AA'.

In our example, the pure polecat-coloured ferrets would be designated as 'AA' (showing that both sets of genes are the same and that albino is recessive to polecat), while that of the albino is assigned the code 'aa'. Geneticists also use their own method to simplify the way that calculations are carried out. The principle is exactly the same as that used by mathematicians when working out problems involving numbers. The method is known as the 'punnett square', and involves the letters representing each set of genes being written along one side and the top of the square. These are then added together to give the answers in each square.

Male Genes (Pure Polecat)

		P	P
Female Genes	P	PP	PP
(Pure Polecat)	P	PP	PP

Male Genes (Pure Polecat)

		A	A
Female Genes	a	Aa	Aa
(Pure Albino)	a	Aa	Aa

Where a dominant gene (ie one denoted by an upper case letter) is present, it will be this that dictates the phenotype of the ferret. Therefore, in both of the foregoing examples, all progeny would be phenotypically polecat. The resultant young of the mating of two pure polecat-coloured ferrets have identical genes (ie P and P) and are said to be homozygous for polecat coloration; but the progeny of the mating between the polecat-coloured ferret and the albino have a gene from the polecat (A) and one from the albino (a), and are said to be heterozygous (or 'split') for albino.

If these splits are now self mated (ie mated brother to sister), we will see that the recessive genes will now have a chance to show themselves.

Male Genes (splits)

		A	a
Female Genes	A	AA	Aa
(splits)	a	Aa	aa

Obviously, those ferrets carrying the 'aa' genotype will have the phenotype of the albino while those carrying 'AA' and 'Aa' will have a polecat type phenotype. In all such matings (ie between two splits both with the same genotype) *approximately* twenty-five per cent of the litter will show the recessive gene in their appearance. This is often expressed as '25:50:25', or '1:2:1' to show the proportions of different genotypes that one would *theoretically* expect to get in the litter. However, it should be noted that any percentages given in genetics are based on the same principles as statistics, and therefore only approximate; to achieve these types of figures, huge numbers must be bred. This phenomenon will never be more apparent than in a litter from a mating that only produces a single kit; obviously, whichever phenotype that kit displayed, the actual percentages would one hundred per cent of one and zero per cent of the others!

If one mated a split with its recessive parent, the litter would contain fifty per cent splits (ie phenotypically polecat) and fifty per cent pure albinos.

Another way of illustrating inheritance involving two ferrets of different genotypes is as follows;

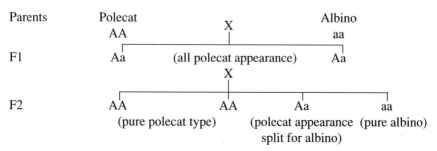

Parents	Polecat AA	X	Albino aa
F1	Aa	(all polecat appearance) X	Aa
F2	AA (pure polecat type)	AA	Aa (polecat appearance split for albino)	aa (pure albino)

The principles outlined above are very important for breeding good stock and 'crossing' to improve a specific line. For example, if you have a line of polecat-coloured ferrets where all of the animals are of good type and size, but have a line of albinos that do not possess these qualities, you can mate one variety to the other, knowing that, within two generations, you would again be producing pure bred animals.

Di-hybrid Inheritance

The story is complicated when *both* parents are splits — but not for the same colours. The calculations to solve this problem are carried out in exactly the same way as previous calculations, ie with the use of a punnett square. No matter how experienced you may get, you will never be wasting your time by drawing a punnett square and working out all of the possibilities on paper, rather than relying totally on mental arithmetic.

Although very little work has been carried out on ferret genetics, or at least on the coat colour inheritance, we know from the results of the breeding of other species that some colours and varieties cannot be produced by 'mixing' others; it is necessary to have one or more animals which are actually carrying the specific mutant gene. Other varieties, however, are obtained from a mix and consequent combination of genes.

Many people speak glibly of 'polecat' and 'albino' colorations in ferrets; however, if these were the only two genotypes, we would not be able to produce all of the other varieties that are so common today. The exception to this statement is the black-eyed white. Every black-eyed white that I have seen has been the result of careful breeding (using inbreeding) to eliminate all dark hairs in the ferret leaving an almost white animal with black eyes. I am told that some breeders have found the mutant gene which creates a true black-eyed white, but I have never seen such an animal. I have, however, seen white ferrets with very dark (ruby) eyes.

Geneticists have discovered many genes which produce a 'white' animal, and only one gene that produces the true albino. Remember that the term albino means an animal completely lacking in pigmentation, ie it has no colour whatsoever; its fur is pure white, and its eyes are opaque, although the blood seen through the eyes gives them a pink appearance. What then of the 'yellow' ferrets? While some will tell you that these are merely the result of albinos being kept in dirty conditions (and with some animals this may be true), careful examination of these yellow ferrets will reveal that the fur has its own colour, and the eyes are not opaque, but pink. When crossed with a polecat-coloured ferret, many of the offspring appear to be normal polecat-coloured animals.

However, if one looks at these very closely, certain differences appear. Some of the guard hairs are now 'white'; certain points of the body (eg feet, chest and top of head) are also 'white'. The most important difference, however, is slightly more difficult to see; the eyes have a dark red tinge to them, and this is known to geneticists as a ruby eye. The coloration will only show under certain lighting, and this is why many owners have never noticed the colour difference. Such an animal is known by many different terms — silver sable, white-mitt, sandy etc.

It is the presence of these 'other' white genes which appears to be giving the ferret world such a profusion of varieties at present. I am, however, certain that, as more ferrets are bred, more mutant alleles will be found, and the number of varieties will increase dramatically.

Sex Linked Inheritance

It will be remembered that it is the male ferret who has both an X and a Y chromosome (XY), while the female has two X chromosomes (XX). If a mutation occurs on either of these two sex chromosomes, it is referred to as 'sex linked'.

In most species, the most obvious example of such a gene is the one which is responsible for both the tortoiseshell and the yellow varieties — To — and it extends the yellow pigment in the fur. In a homozygous animal (ToTo), this will result in a yellow coat, while in a heterozygous (Toto), it will give rise to a tortoiseshell variety. This occurs because of the presence of one normal X chromosome which will limit the effect of that chromosome carrying the TO gene, and the yellow colouring will therefore be restricted. For this reason, normally only female tortoiseshells will ever appear, but both male and female yellows will appear. *Very* occasionally, a male tortoiseshell will appear, but these are invariably infertile.

Lethal and Semi-lethal Genes

In some mutations, if the foetus has a double helping of that particular gene, ie they are homozygous, the animal dies. These are known as lethal genes. It is not known if any such genes occur in the ferret, although the likelihood is that they do. When these are seen, it can safely be assumed that the animals are heterozygous and, when either of these two varieties are bred together, there will be a one in four chance of any of the resultant foetuses having a homozygous combination of these genes; they will, therefore, die while in the womb, being re-absorbed. Their siblings who survive will not, please note, suffer any adverse effects from the lethal gene. They will also all be splits, as it is obviously never possible to pure breed these varieties.

Research

We all need to discover more about the ferret's genetic make-up; one of my biggest disappointments while researching this book was my failure to find any scientific and valid results on the genetics of the ferret. This was not due to my short comings — many though they are — but to the complete lack of such material.

I am sure that you, like me, will find it absolutely amazing that, after having kept ferrets in captivity for so many years, we have not obtained any information on such a basic subject. Even those individuals and companies who have (and still are) breeding ferrets for their pelts — and would obviously benefit from scientific facts regarding coat colour inheritance — have failed to keep proper records, or at least to communicate the results of their breeding programmes. It is a sad state of affairs, and one that should be addressed as soon as possible by all with a real interest in the ferret — for whatever reason.

You, the reader, can help, simply by keeping accurate records of all breeding carried out. A central body could easily collate this data, and reach conclusions which will help us all. The UK's National Ferret School has agreed to act in this manner, and all interested parties should contact them for further details. (See Appendix 4).

Appendix 1

Ferret Facts and Figures

The ferret's skeleton. Note the slender rib-cage

Average weight (adult)	Between 400g and 2kg.
Average size (adult)	Between 35cm and 60cm (hob up to twice size of jill).
Average life-span (in captivity)	Between eight and twelve years.
Age at puberty	250 days (approx).
Age at sexual maturity	Eight to twelve months (spring after birth).
Normal breeding season (Britain)	Early March to late September.

Number of chromosomes	Forty (twenty pairs).
Breeding Season	Triggered by photoperiod — requires longer days than nights.
First possible mating	Six months.
Duration of oestrus	Ceases when mated; if unmated, will continue to end of 'season' (can last for six months), often causing medical problems.
Signs of oestrus	Vulva swells, becomes vivid pink colour, with secretion. In male, testes swell and descend into scrotum.
Duration of mating	Several hours.
Ovulation	About thirty hours after coitus.
Reduction of vulva	Begins seven to ten days after mating; complete within two to three weeks.
Palpation	Ten days after vulva totally reduced.
Gestation (pregnancy)	Forty to forty-four days (average 42 days).
Number of young (in one litter)	One to fifteen (average six to eight). Jills can have up to two litters per year. Largest litter ever recorded — fifteen.
Litters per year	Under normal conditions, one or two; with extra lighting (ie adjustment of photoperiod) up to five.
Post-natal oestrus	One to two weeks after weaning.
Weight at birth	Five to fifteen grams.
State at birth	Blind, deaf, naked and entirely dependant upon the mother.
Ears/eyes open	Twenty-two to thirty-six days.
Fur	In dark coloured kits, starts to appear within five to seven days. Good covering by four weeks.
Deciduous teeth	Erupt at ten to fourteen days.
Canine teeth	Forty-seven to fifty-two days.
Movement	Kits as young as two to three weeks will manage to crawl out of nest (to be dragged back by the mother).
Weaning	Seven to nine weeks.
Weight at weaning	300g — 500g.
Age attain adult weight	Four to five months.
Minimum selling/buying age	Twelve weeks.
Rectal temperature	38.6°C (Range 37.8° — 40°C).
Heart Rate	220 — 250bpm.
Respiratory rate	30 — 40 per minute.
Number of toes	Five per foot.

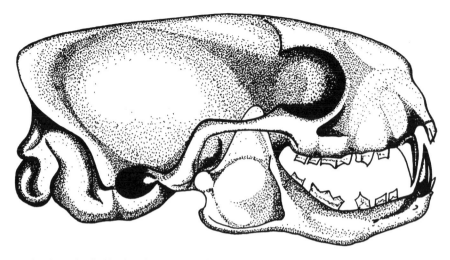

The ferret's skull, clearly showing the large canine teeth for which the animal is renowned.

Teeth	Incisors 3/3, canines 1/1, premolars 3/3, molars 1/2.
Nipples	Two rows of four (eight in total) — on both sexes.
Vertebrae	C7, T14, L6, S3, COL14—18, 14 pairs of ribs.
Other anatomy	No appendix, caecum, or male prostate gland. Under-developed sweat glands.
Sexing	Ano-genital distance of female half that of male.

Appendix 2

Glossary of Ferret and Ferreting Terms

Albino
A white ferret, with no pigmentation in its flesh or eyes. The eyes are opaque but, due to the fact that blood can be seen behind the eyes, they appear pink. There are several other types of white ferrets which are *not* albinos.

Austringer
The traditional term for one who keeps and hunts hawks.

Autosomes
Chromosomes other than those which determine the sex of the progeny of a mating.

Bedding
The material supplied to ferrets for their nest. Top quality meadow hay is best; do not use cotton wool, newspaper or any long-fibred synthetic material.

Benching
The act of placing ferrets on the show-bench, for the attention of the judge officiating at that show.

Business
The collective term for a group of ferrets.

Cage
The container in which ferrets are kept. These can be commercially manufactured or home-made by breeders using wood, plastic or metal.
(See also 'Court' and 'Cub')

Canines
The front teeth of a ferret which it uses to kill its prey.

Carbohydrates
Food constituents which provide the body with food and material for growth.

Cannibalism
The killing and eating of one ferret by another ferret.

Carrying-box
A container designed to hold one or more ferrets, ideal for travelling or transporting the ferrets to and from a

	show, race or working area. Sometimes called a travelling-box.
Chromosomes	Thread-like bodies, carried inside the nucleus of every germ-cell, which carry the genes of the individual animal.
Classes	At a ferret show, entries are divided into classes, to facilitate judging. These classes are usually dictated by colour, variety or sex of the ferret concerned.
Coitus	The physical act of mating.
Collar	A collar is placed around the neck of the liner ferret and a line attached to it. Pet ferrets are often put on to a collar and lead and taken for walks!
Cope	A metal muzzle. (See also 'muzzle')
Court	A traditional type of cage, rather like an aviary, in which ferrets are kept.
Colony	Term used to describe the keeping of a group of ferrets together, usually for commercial breeding purposes, where one male is kept with several females.
Crepuscular	The term used to describe an animal that is active around the hours of dusk and dawn.
Cub	The traditional name for the hutch-like cage in which some ferrets are kept.
Culling	The removal and killing of some kits in a litter which is thought to be too large for the mother to rear. This is totally unnecessary, as the female ferret will know her own limits, culling the litter as she sees fit, starting with the weakest members.
Dam	The mother of a litter.
Dominant	A gene which will always show itself in the phenotype of a ferret, even if there is only one of these genes present. Such genes are denoted by the use of an upper case (capital) letter.

Ectoparasite	A parasite which lives on the outside of the host animal eg fleas, lice and ticks. (See also 'Parasite' and 'Endoparasite')
Electronic Detector	A device for tracking ferrets (and terriers), used while ferrets are working underground. The device consists of a collar-mounted transmitter (worn by the ferret or terrier) and a hand-held receiver. Both are pre-tuned. A modern detector can be used to a depth of almost eight feet (2.44 metres).
Endoparasite	A parasite that lives inside the host animal (eg in the intestines etc.) such as tapeworms. (See also 'Parasite' and 'Ectoparasite')
Fats	Constituents of food which provide the ferret's body with energy. A surplus of fats in a ferret's diet will cause it to become overweight, with danger to its health. This is even more so if the ferret is also deprived of sufficient exercise.
Ferret	The domesticated European polecat *(Mustella putorius)*. The term is often (erroneously) used to describe only the albino version of this species.
Ferret Detector	(see 'Electronic detector')
Fibre	The indigestible material present in some foods which helps stimulate the action of the intestines. Used to be known as 'roughage'.
Fitch	The ferret's fur.
Fitchet	A term used to describe the offspring of a mating between a polecat and an albino ferret — the term was originally used to describe the young of a *wild* polecat and a domesticated ferret, but today it is used for the progeny of any mating between a coloured polecat (or ferret) and an albino ferret.
Foot-rot	A disease caused by mites and resulting in the feet of the afflicted ferret quite literally rotting. Once thought to be caused solely by the ferrets being kept in dirty and wet conditions.

Gene	A hereditary factor of inherited material. Genes are carried on the chromosome.
Genetics	The study of the ways in which certain characteristics are passed on from one generation to the next.
Genitals (Genitalia)	The external sex organs of a ferret.
Genotype	The genetic make-up of a ferret.
Genus	A group of animals containing species which closely resemble each other, eg the weasel tribe (*Mustelidae*).
Germ-cell	The egg of a female and the sperm of the male ferret.
Gestation	Pregnancy. In ferrets, this is between forty and forty-four days, usually forty-two.
Greyhound Ferret	A tiny, agile ferret. Sometimes referred to as a 'whippet ferret'.
Heat	A term often used to describe oestrus.
Heatstroke	The effect of too much heat on a ferret. If this condition is not treated, it can be fatal. Sometimes referred to as 'the sweats'.
Hob	A male ferret or polecat.
Hobble	A castrated hob.
Hoblet	A vasectomized hob.
Hospital Cage	A special cage for sick or injured ferrets. It is fitted with a thermostatically controlled heater.
Hybrid	A cross-bred ferret, ie heterozygous. The term can either mean the offspring of a wild polecat and a domesticated ferret or the progeny of a mating of a closely-bred animal and a completely unrelated one.
Hybrid Vigour	The increased vigour and resistance to disease often found in the offspring resulting from the mating of completely unrelated ferrets.

In-breeding	The practice of breeding very closely related ferrets together. (See also 'line breeding')
Incinerator	A device for burning rubbish (especially soiled shavings and bedding). Essential for the safe disposal of bedding and shavings etc from the cages of infected and ill ferrets.
Incisors	The front teeth of a ferret.
Inheritance	The manner in which certain characteristics are passed from one generation to the next.
Intractability	Lack of tameness; impossible to handle without the risk of being bitten.
Jill	A female ferret or polecat.
Kit or Kitten	A young ferret, usually used to describe a ferret of 16 weeks of age or less (the same terms are also used to describe young rabbits). Comes from the name of the young of the polecat, ie pole-kitten!
Life Expectancy	(See 'Longevity')
Line	A 'family' of ferrets, bred for several generations.
Line Breeding	A moderate form of inbreeding.
Litter	The young ferrets produced at one birth.
Locus	Position on a chromosomes occupied by a specific gene (Plural locii)
Longevity	Length of life. In the ferret, this is about eight to twelve years in captivity. The oldest ferret that I have ever known was 'Izzy', a poley jill, who was almost fourteen years of age at the time of her death.
Mask	The markings on the face of a polecat (or polecat ferret). This mask is usually darker in the summer than in the winter.
Mating	(See 'Coitus')

Minerals	Minute constituents of a ferret's diet, without which he will not have a balanced diet, with a consequent adverse effect on his health.
Monohybrid Inheritance	The inheritance of a single characteristic.
Musk	The foul smelling scent produced by the anal glands of ferrets and polecats.
Mutant or Mutant Allele	The changed gene which results in a change in an animal.
Muzzle	A device for preventing the ferret from biting (either humans or his natural quarry). Made from leather, string or metal; they must *never* be used on ferrets while they are working. Also the name for the ferret's nose.
Myxomatosis	A deadly viral disease amongst rabbits. Thought to have been deliberately introduced to the UK from France, to 'control' the numbers of wild rabbits.
Nocturnal	The term used to describe an animal that is active by night, sleeping by day.
Oestrus	The state in which a jill will accept a mating. (See also 'Heat')
Oestrous Cycle	The sexual cycle of a female ferret.
Overshot	A jaw whose upper incisors overlap those on the bottom of the jaw.
Ovulation	The release of eggs into the womb to be fertilised by the hob's sperm.
Parasites	Animals which live on or in other animals (hosts) in a manner which is detrimental to the host. Includes worms, fleas, mites, lice and ticks. (See also 'endoparasites' and 'ectoparasites')
Paunch	(Verb) To remove the 'guts' of a rabbit. (Noun) An animal's stomach.
Pen	An old fashioned term for a cage.

Phenotype	The physical appearance of a ferret.
Photoperiodism	The dependence on the daytime/night-time (or simply light and dark) ratio of various biological functions, particularly the commencement of oestrus.
Polecat	The common name of the animal *Mustela putorius*. Strictly, this name should only be used to describe the wild polecat, but today it is also commonly used to describe *any* domesticated ferret with polecat type markings. The name originates from the French 'Poule Chat' — chicken cat!
Poley	A domesticated ferret with the typical wild polecat markings.
Pregnancy	(See 'Gestation')
Proteins	The basic constituents of all living things and an essential constituent of a balanced diet; essential for growth and tissue maintenance.
Quiet	The term used to describe an easy-to-handle ferret.
Recessive	A gene which is masked unless another identical gene is present in a ferret. Such genes are denoted by writing their code in lower case letters.
Records	All of the information concerning your ferrets. These records must always be kept and, of course, kept accurately.
Roughage	An old-fashioned term for fibre.
Sandy	A coloured ferret with colouring between an albino and a polecat.
Scours	Diarrhoea.
Season	(See 'Oestrus')
Sex Chromosomes	The chromosomes responsible for determining the sex of a ferret. Males have one X chromosome and one Y. Females have a pair of X chromosomes. All other chromosomes are known as autosomes.

Sex Linked	The term used to describe a characteristic where the mutant inheritance allele is carried on the sex chromosome and is, therefore, governed by the sex of the individual.
Sexual Dimorphism	The differences exhibited between the sexes, eg the male ferret always has the capacity to grow larger than the female (up to twice the size).
Sibling	Brother or sister; litter mate.
Sire	The father of a litter.
Skulk	When a ferret refuses to leave the mouth of a tunnel or its nest-box/cage, it is said to be 'skulking'.
Sops	Bread and milk, sometimes (though wrongly) fed to ferrets.
Split	The term used to describe a ferret whose parents were of different colours.
Sport	The term used to indicate a ferret that is genetically different from the norm.
Stud	An individual ferret 'kennel', where ferrets are bred. Some clubs allow one to register a stud prefix (name) which is exclusive to the registrant. Often used to describe the male ferret used for breeding purposes.
Stud-book	The record (not necessarily a book) of all of the ferrets in a particular stud.
Sweats	(See 'Heatstroke')
Terrarium	Cage.
Travelling-box	(See 'Carrying-box')
Undershot	A jaw whose lower incisors overlap those on the top jaw.
Variety	A specific colour and coat type of the ferret, eg silver sable.

Vaccination	An injection of a mild form of a specific pathogenic micro-organism, which causes the body to form antibodies, thus helping to prevent the treated animal from acquiring a full dose of the specific disease, eg distemper.
Virus	Bacteria able to cause disease.
Vitamin Deficiency	The lack of certain important vitamins; this term is usually used to indicate the result of such a deficiency, rather than the actual lack of the vitamin(s) in question.
Vitamins	Organic compounds, essential to the health of a ferret. Usually referred to by letters of the alphabet, eg A, B, C, etc.
Water Bottle	The bottle, equipped with a stainless steel spout, in which a ferret is supplied with water. Every ferret must have access to clear, clean, fresh water at all times.
Weaning	The development of the eating habits of ferret kits when they progress from being dependent upon their mothers for food, and are capable of feeding themselves, ie eating solid food.
Zoonose or Zoonotic Disease	Disease capable of being transmitted from animals to humans, eg salmonellosis.
Zygote	A fertilised egg.

Appendix 3

Bibliography

The inclusion of a title does not infer any endorsement by the author; neither does the omission of a title infer lack of approval.

All About Ferrets
Mervin F. Roberts
Publishers — TFH (1977)

The Amateur Poacher
Richard Jefferies
Publishers — Oxford University Press (1879)

Animal Tracks and Traces
Miroslav Bouchner
Publishers — Octopus (1982)

Animal Traps and Trapping
J.A. Bateman
Publishers — David and Charles (1971)

The Art of Ferreting
Owen Jones and Marcus Woodward
Publishers — Derbyshire Museum Service

The Art of Long-netting
Harold Wyman
Publishers — Dickson Price (1989)

Biology and Diseases of the Ferret
James G. Fox
Publishers — Lea and Febiger (1988)

Black's Veterinary Dictionary
Edited by Geoffrey West
Publishers — A. and C. Black (1988)

Britain's Wildlife, Plants and Flowers
Publishers — Reader's Digest (1984)

British Mammals
L. Harrison Matthews
Publishers — Collins (1968)

The Brown Rat
Graham Twigg
Publishers — David and Charles (1975)

The Carnivores
R.F. Ewer
Publishers — Weidenfeld and Nicolson (1973)

The Complete Book of Ferrets
Val Porter and Nicholas Brown
Publishers — Pelham Books (1985)

The Complete Jack Russell Terrier
David Brian Plummer
Publishers — Boydell (1980)

Common and Endangered Mammals of the UK
John Gale
Publishers — Dryad Press (1987)

Conservation Biology and the Black-Footed Ferret
Editors — Ulysses S. Seal, E. Tom Thorne, Michael A. Bogan, and
Stanley H Anderson
Publishers — York University Press (1989)

Colour Inheritance in Small Livestock
Roy Robinson
Publishers — Fur & Feather (1978)

The Domestication and Exploitation of Plants and Animals
P.J. Ucko
Publishers — Duckworth

The Encyclopedia of Mammals Volume 1
Edited by Dr David MacDonald
Publishers — Guild (1985)

The Evolution of Domesticated Animals
Edited by I.L. Mason
Publishers — Longman (1984)

Fair Game
Charlie Parkes and John Thornley
Publishers — Pelham Books (1987)

Falconry
Jemima Parry-Jones
Publishers — David and Charles (1993)

Falconry and Hawking
Phillip Glasier
Publishers — BT Batsford (1978)

Falconry Art and Practice
Emma Ford
Publishers — Blandford (1992)

The Ferret and Ferreting Guide
Graham Welstead
Publishers — David and Charles (1981)

The Ferret & Ferreting Handbook
James McKay
Publishers — The Crowood Press (1989)

Ferreting and Trapping for Amateur Keepers
Guy N. Smith
Publishers — Spur Publications (1979)

Ferrets
Jay and Mary Field
Publishers — TFH (1987)

Ferrets
Wendy Winstead
Publishers — TFH (1981)

Ferrets — A Complete Pet Owner's Manual
Chuck and Fox Morton
Publishers — Barron's (1985)

Ferrets and Ferreting
Iain Brodie
Publishers — Blandford (1978)

Ferrets and Ferreting
W. Carnegie *et al*
Publishers — Nimrod Press (1988)

Ferrets and Ferreting
Peter Whitaker
Publishers — Pugs and Drummers (1978)

Ferrets in Your Home
Wendy Winstead
Publishers — TFH (1990)

Ferrets — Their Management in Health and Disease
N. Everitt
Publishers — N. Everitt (1897)

Field Guide to the Animals of Britain
Publishers — Reader's Digest (1984)

First-aid for Animals
Piero Fortunati
Publishers — Sidgwick & Jackson (1989)

Full Revelations of a Professional Ratcatcher
Ike Williams
Publishers — Nimrod Press (1988)

The Gamekeeper at Home
Richard Jefferies
Publishers — Oxford University Press (1878)

Guide to Ferreting
Fred J. Taylor
Publishers — Buchan and Enright (1983)

The Guinness Encyclopedia of the Living World
Ed — B. Gardiner & P. Moore
Publishers — Guinness Publishing (1992)

Grzimek's Animal Life Encyclopedia (Vols 10, 11 and 12)
Edited by B. Grzimek
Publishers — Van Nostrand Reinhold (1972)

The Handbook of British Mammals (3rd ed)
Ed — G.B. Corbet and S. Harris
Publishers — Blackwell Scientific Publications (1991)

The Handbook of British Mammals
H.N. Southern
Publishers — The Mammal Society

Handbook of Shooting
Edited by Gerry D. Turner
Publishers — Pelham Books, in conjunction with the British Association for Shooting and Conservation

In Pursuit of Coney
David Brian Plummer
Publishers — Boydell (1991)

An Introduction to Animal Law
Margaret Cooper, LLB
Publishers — The Academic Press (1987)

An Introduction to Veterinary Anatomy and Physiology
A.R. Michell and P.E. Watkins
Publishers — British Small Animal Veterinary Association (1993)

The Jack Russell Terrier
David Brian Plummer
Publishers — Tideline Books (1981)

Jones' Animal Nursing
Edited by R.S. Pinniger
Publishers — Pergamon Press (1972)

The Keepers' Book
A. Stodart Walker and P. Jeffrey Mackie
Publishers — T.N. Foulis (1907)

The Life of Mammals (Vols 1 and 2)
L. Harrison Matthews
Publishers — Weidenfeld and Nicolson (1971)

The Life of Vertebrates
J.Z. Young
Publishers — Oxford University Press (1978)

Mammal Species of the World
J.H. Honacki and K.E. Kinman
Publishers — Allen Press (1982)

The Mammals
Desmond Morris
Publishers — Hodder and Stoughton (1965)

Mammals of Britain — Their Tracks, Trails and Signs
M.J. Lawrence and R.W. Brown
Publishers — Blandford Press (1967)

Management of Canids and Mustelids
Proceedings of the 5th Symposium of the Association of British Wild Animal Keepers
Publishers — (ABWAK) (1980)

Manual of Exotic Pets
Editors J.E. Cooper, M.F. Hutchinson, O.F. Jackson and R.J. Maurice
Publishers — The British Small Animal Veterinary Association (1992)

Mink
Johnny Birks
Publishers — The Mammal Society (1986)

Modern Ferreting
David Brian Plummer
Publishers — Boydell Press (1977)

A Natural History of Domesticated Animals
Juliet Clutton-Brock
Publishers — Cambridge University Press and the British Museum (Natural History) (1987)

The Naturalised Animals of the British Isles
Christopher Lever
Publishers — Hutchinson and Co. (1977)

The New Poacher's Handbook
Ian Niall
Publishers — Heinemann (1960)

The Parson and Jack Russell Terriers
Jean and Frank Jackson
Publishers — Popular Dogs (1991)

The Poacher's Handbook
Ian Niall
Publishers — Heinemann (1950)

Practical Pest Control
George Hogg
Publishers — Boydell (1986)

Practical Trapping
W. Carnegie
Publishers — The Bazaar Exchange and Mart

Practical Trapping of Vermin and Birds
W. Carnegie
Publishers — Tideline Books (1975)

Predator Control
Publishers — The Game Conservancy (1994)

Predatory Mammals in Britain (1988)
Edited by Pat Gouldsbury
Publishers — The Council for Nature, London

The Private Life of the Rabbit
R.M. Lockley
Publishers — Andre Deutsch (1965)

Pugs and Drummers
John Marchington
Publishers — Faber and Faber (1978)

The Rabbit
A.E.T. Watson
Publishers — Ashford Press (1986)

The Rabbit
J.E. Harting
Publishers — The Field (1986)

Rabbit Control
The Game Conservancy
Publishers — MAFF and the Game Conservancy (1980)

Rabbits and their History
John Sheill
Publishers — David and Charles

Rabbit Shooting to Ferrets
William Thomas
Publishers — Hutchinson's (1945)

Rabbiting
Bob Smithson
Publishers — The Crowood Press (1988)

Rabbiting and Ferreting
E. Samuel and J. Ivester Lloyd
Publishers — The British Field Sports Society (1966)

Rare Mammals of the World
John Burton and Bruce Pearson
Publishers — Collins (1987)

Rat Catching
H.C. Barkley
Publishers — John Murray (1896)

Ratting and Rabbiting for Amateur Keepers
Guy N. Smith
Publishers — Spur Publications (1979)

RSPCA Book of British Mammals
Editor — C.L. Boyle
Publishers — Collins (1981)

The Shooting Times Guide to Ferreting
Fred J. Taylor
Publishers — Buchan and Enright (1983)

The Sporting Terrier
David Brian Plummer
Publishers — Boydell (1992)

Stoats & Weasels, Polecats & Martens
Paddy Sleeman
Publishers — Whittet Books (1989)

Tales of a Rat-Hunting Man
David Brian Plummer
Publishers — The Boydell Press (1978)

The UFAW Handbook on the Care and Management of Laboratory Animals
Edited by the Universities Federation for Animal Welfare (UFAW)
Publishers — Churchill Livingstone (1976)

The Vanishing Wildlife of Britain
Brian Vesey-FitzGerald
Publishers — MacGibbon & Kee (1969)

The Velvet Claw
David MacDonald
Publishers — BBC Books (1992)

Walker's Mammals of the World
Nowak Pardiso
Publishers — Johns Hopkins University Press (1991)

Weasels and Stoats
Carolyn King
Publishers — Christopher Helm (1989)

A Weasel in my Meatsafe
Phil Drabble
Publishers — William Collins (1957)

Weasels, Badgers, Civets and Mongooses and their Relatives
Publishers — IUCN (International Union for Conservation of Nature and Natural Resources) (1991)

Wild Animals in Britain
Frances Pitt
Publishers — Batsford (1938)

The Wild Rabbit
David Cowan
Publishers — Blandford Press (1980)

Wildlife Rangers' Handbook
Ed — G.D. Springthorpe and N.G. Myhill
Publishers — Forestry Commission (1985)

The Working Jack Russell Terrier
Eddie Chapman
Publishers — Chapman (1985)

A World List of Mammalian Species
G.B. Corbet and J.E. Hill
Publishers — The British Museum (Natural History) (1980)

The Year of the Weasel
Paul Thomas
Publishers — Souvenir Press (1986)

Your First Ferret
Adelle Porch
Publishers — TFH (1991)

Zoology
M.S. Gordon
Publishers — Macmillan (1976)

Appendix 4

Useful Addresses

The following were all correct at the time of going to press; however, details and officers do change, especially where the organisation is a voluntary one. In all cases, where a reply is required, always enclose a stamped self-addressed envelope with all enquiries.

The inclusion of an organisation does not imply any standard or the author's approval of that organisation; neither does the exclusion of any organisation imply any disapproval. I have written to every ferret and ferreting organisation that I can obtain details of — throughout the world — and have published requests for information concerning such organisations in newspapers and magazines. Unfortunately, many of my requests went unheeded, and that is the main reason for not including some organisations. Even more infuriating were the number of replies which gave the names of the organisation and every committee member and officer, yet failed to give any address! Such organisations have not, for obvious reasons, been included!

Germany
Erste Interessengemeinschaft Frettchenfreunde Hessen
Friedberger Strasse 98
6368 Bad Vilbel 1

Frettchen Club Berlin
Fuchsienweg 18A
D-1000 Berlin 47

Frettchen und Iltisclub NRW
Wehringhauser Strasse 79
5800 Hagen 1

Frettchen und Marderclub Deutschland
Eifelweg 16
30851 Langenhagen

Frettchen Zuchtverband
Dorf Strasse 26
0-1401 Teschendorf

Frettchenfreunde NRW
In der Grossen Heide 6
44339 Dortmund

Netherlands
Stichting de Fret
Boteronstraat 41
1445 LH Purmerend
Holland

Norway
Norsk Tamilder Forening
Kastellvcien 20
1162 Oslo 11

Sweden
Stif Vast/Svenska Tam-Iller Foreningen
Norra Barsjov 19
427 35 Lindome

This organisation has many local groups, details of which can be obtained from the above address.

Switzerland
S.F.F.S.
Hardstr. 41
CH-5432 Neuenhof

United Kingdom
British Association for Shooting and Conservation
(formerly known as WAGBI)
Marford Mill
Rossett
Wrexham
Clwyd LL12 0HL

An organisation which, although not specifically for ferrets and ferreters, does work to encourage and maintain shooting sports; as such, ferreting interests are represented within the Association.

British Falconers' Club
Home Farm
Tamworth
Staffordshire
B78 3DW

British Field Sports Society
59 Kennington Road
London
SE1 7PZ

An organisation which represents the interests of all country sports, including ferreting.

British School of Falconry
Stelling Minnis
Canterbury
Kent

Deben Group Industries
Deben Way
Melton
Woodbridge
Suffolk
IP12 1RB

Manufacturers of ferret detectors and other electronic equipment.

The East Anglian Ferret Welfare Association
35 Lamborne Gardens
Hornchurch, Essex
RM12 4LJ

The Essex Ferret Welfare Society
21 Moreton Road
Shelley
Ongar
Essex
CM5 0AP

The Ferret Roadshow
PO Box 61
Chesterfield
Derbyshire
S42 6ZX

Formed by the author in 1982, the Ferret Roadshow is the mobile arm of the National Ferret School and travels throughout the UK giving displays and lectures on all aspects of ferrets and ferreting.

The Game Conservancy
Fordingbridge
Hampshire
SP6 1EF

The Gem Ferret Care Group
24 Arden Road
Furnace Green
Crawley
West Sussex
RH10 6HS

The Hawk and Owl Trust
c/o The Birds of Prey Section
London Zoo
London
NW1 4RY

The Kent Ferret Welfare Society
5 Eastern Gardens
Willesborough
Ashford
Kent
TN24 0HE

Males
Warners Lane
Selsey
West Sussex
PO20 9EL

Manufacturers of live-catch mink traps, ideal for capturing ferrets.

The National Database of Ferret-Friendly Vets
PO Box 61
Chesterfield
Derbyshire
S42 6ZX

A computer database, established by the author, of veterinary surgeons who have experience or interest in ferrets and their ailments. Addition to the database is free and enquiries providing a stamped self-addressed envelope are also free.

The National Ferret School
PO Box 61
Chesterfield
Derbyshire
S42 6ZX

This organisation, of which the author is founder, runs courses on all aspects of ferrets and ferreting. Fact and information sheets are also issued by the school, which issued a Code of Conduct for Organisers of Ferret Racing and Displays (See Appendix 5). Please send a stamped self-addressed envelope with all enquiries, stating full details of your requirements or enquiry.

The National Ferret Welfare Society
6 St Edmund Road
Bedford
MK40 2NQ

The Scottish Ferret Club
37 Tutor Road
Leuchars
St Andrews
Fife
KY16 0JW

The South East Ferret Club
Westbury 2
Waterditch Road
Warren Street
Lenham
Kent
ME17 2DY

South Yorkshire Ferrets
57 Adkins Road
Sheffield
S5 8TF

Universities Federation for Animal Welfare
8 Hamilton Close
South Mimms
Potters Bar
Hertfordshire
EN6 3QD

The Wessex Ferret Club
33 Barlows Road
Tadley
Basingstoke
Hampshire
RG26 6NA

United States
The American Ferret Association
PO Box 3986
Frederick
MD 21705

The American Ferret Veterinary Association
1014 Williamson Street
Madison
WI

The Black-footed Ferret Fund
c/o Wyoming Game and Fish Department
5400 Bishop Boulevard
Cheyenne
WY 82002

For information on the progress of the black-footed ferret breeding and re-introduction project, and also to make donations to help the work of protecting the ferret's most endangered relative.

The Ferret Fancier's Club
713 Chautauqua Court
Pittsburgh
PA 15214

Ferret Unity and Registration Organisation (FURO)
PO Box 844
Elon College
North Carolina
27244

Ferret World Inc
6 Water Street
Box 555
Assonet
Massachusetts 02702

Manufacturers and distributors of a wide range of ferret equipment.

The International Ferret Association
PO Box 522
Roanoke
Virginia
24003

Marshall Pet Products
5740 Limekiln Road
Wolcott
New York
14590

The largest breeders of ferrets in the USA.

The Miami Ferret Club Inc.
19225 SW 93rd Road
Miami
Florida
33157

Appendix 5

Code of Conduct for Organisers of Ferret Racing and Displays

Ferret displays, involving racing and other activities, are now extremely common — and rightly popular — at all major country shows and other events throughout the British Isles, and in many other countries. It is important to remember that these ferret displays are the public image of ferrets and ferret keeping, and it makes sense, therefore, to ensure that ferret keepers, clubs and others with an interest in the subject are seen in the best light.

All too often, ferrets used in displays are not treated correctly and, as a result, both ferrets and members of the public are put at risk — sometimes even injured. All it takes is one serious incident, and all ferret owners will suffer the consequences. This code of conduct consists of commonsense practices and precautions which are designed to ensure that accidents do not occur — to either ferrets or humans — and that ferrets used in displays are treated correctly. It is in everyone's interests that all adhere to this code.

The Organisers of Ferret Racing and Displays Should;

1. Ensure that the well-being of the ferrets is paramount and is given the highest priority at all times; no ferret should be used too often, nor made to endure any treatment that may result in injury or stress, to either ferret or human.

2. Ensure that the ferrets are transported to and from the event in suitable caging, with due regard to temperature regulation, and in full compliance with all Transport of Animals Orders.

3. Ensure that, except when actually participating in racing or similar activities, the ferrets have constant access to suitable food, water and shelter.

4. Ensure that, except when actually participating in racing or similar activities, the ferrets are kept in cages of appropriate size and construction, allowing shelter from extremes of temperature and prevailing weather conditions.

5. Ensure that the ferrets receive regular veterinary treatment and vaccinations, as necessary.

6. Ensure that the ferrets are accompanied at all times while on site, and one person should be given overall responsibility for the ferrets' welfare while on site; their guidance should be sought before any activity involving the ferrets.

7. Be registered under the Performing Animals (Regulation) Act, 1925.

8. Hold public liability insurance to a minimum of £1M.

9. Ensure conformance with health and safety guide-lines, and adherence with the Code of Conduct of the Council for Environmental Education.

10. Ensure that at least one member of the team on site holds a recognised first-aid qualification, and that suitable first-aid equipment (for both animals and humans) is available at all times.

For further information, please contact the National Ferret School,
PO Box 61, Chesterfield, Derbyshire S42 6ZX

© James McKay 1995.
The National Ferret School, All Rights Reserved.

Index